The
ANTIQUES ROADSHOW
QUIZ BOOK

The
ANTIQUES ROADSHOW
QUIZ BOOK

Compiled by
Judith & Martin Miller

BRITISH BROADCASTING
CORPORATION

CHILSTON PUBLICATIONS

Published by the British Broadcasting
Corporation
35 Marylebone High Street,
London W1M 4AA
and Chilston Publications
Sissinghurst Court, Sissinghurst,
Cranbrook, Kent TN17 2JA

First published 1986

ISBN 0 563 20419 2

Printed and bound in Great Britain by
William Clowes Ltd
Beccles and London

Contents

A toy no child is ever likely to play with!
Both dolls have bisque heads and are dressed in contemporary
lace-trimmed clothes. The standing doll contains a clockwork
mechanism to make it walk, pulling the cart along as it does so.
Automata such as this are definitely collectors' items, and this
one was valued in 1985 at £1200-£1800.

Preface by Robin Drake

The Antiques Roadshow Quiz Book will, I hope, be the first of many publications associated with what has proved to be the most popular antiques programme ever devised. The **Roadshow** features regularly in the BBC's top ten with an audience averaging ten million.

The programme is produced from the BBC's Bristol Network Production Centre, which has a first-rate track record for antiques programmes that have delighted beginners and connoisseurs alike over the past twenty years. Programmes such as **Going for a Song, Collectors' World** and **Arthur Negus Enjoys** were all Bristol-produced. **The Antiques Roadshow** is very much a child of those earlier successes.

Reading the vast postbag generated by these programmes left me in no doubt that, whilst the viewers delighted in the very fine and excellent objects in **Going for a Song**, and appreciated the more attainable items in **Collectors' World** there remained a need for a third kind of programme – a programme directly accessible to the viewers to which they could bring, not only their treasures, but also all the questions we found in the postbag.

A programme format was devised with the accent on informality to enable the needs of those attending the recording to be met, as well as providing a programme that entertained, informed and encouraged the viewing audience. To be a success the format had to meet several challenges. Firstly the high technical standards of the studio-based programmes must be maintained in the more difficult Outside Broadcast environment. Secondly we had to promote a first-rate event to bring together the people of a town along with any items on which they would like an expert opinion. We had then to capture this televisually. Finally, the new informal structure must not stand in the way of the need to inform and entertain.

The concept of **The Antiques Roadshow** was put to the test on 17 May 1977 at Hereford Town Hall. I well remember the relief I and all the members of the team felt as the doors opened at 10 a.m. In trooped what seemed to us then like a flood of thirty or so with the now familiar collection of carrier bags, cartons, bin liners and even a plastic dustbin almost concealing a large Satsuma vase. For six hours we hunted through all the items brought in by the 600 or so people who continued to throng through the doors. We found all manner of fascinating items; from a fine pair of Jacobean silver caskets valued at £5000, to late Woolworth valued at 50p. The day was a great success for all concerned and the television series was accepted.

Nine years and over sixty towns later the initial queue of people waiting outside before the show begins can be measured in hundreds rather than tens, and the average attendance throughout the day is around 4000 people. The **Roadshow** team has now travelled as far north as Aberdeen, south to Jersey and Guernsey, west to Aberystwyth and east to Scarborough, in recording eight series. The experts must have seen almost a quarter of a million people bearing nearly a million items. The interesting thing that emerges is that there is still no lack of objects of an almost endless variety for opinion. There are always new finds and surprises, and it has been a pleasure to meet the public and enjoy with them their treasures, and to observe the awakening of an entirely new appreciation of a familiar object that comes with the knowledge of who made it, when, and for what purpose.

The fascination for the programme continues undiminished as we begin a ninth series; some viewers I know treat the valuation element as a parlour game among the family, others write that the identification is all-important and the valuation is merely crude commercialism. I even discovered one group of hardened gamblers who anxiously await the valuation to see who scoops the pot as there are no horses to back on Sunday. This demonstrates the wide appeal of the **Roadshow**. Certainly those who attend and participate at whatever level enjoy the experience. Collecting antiques should be fun, there is satisfaction in ownership, and it is interesting to find out all about an item. And it can be really exciting to discover the true value of some trifle.

The Antiques Roadshow has without doubt given a large number of people great pleasure. The **Quiz Book** will appeal equally to all who enjoy the programme, as it contains the same mix of fun and information as well as the chance to win a valuable prize.

Robin Drake,
Producer, **The Antiques Roadshow**

Introduction

What, exactly, is an antique? Well, according to the Collins Dictionary of the English Language, an antique is: '1: a decorative object, piece of furniture or other work of art created in an earlier period, that is collected and valued for its beauty, workmanship and age. 2: any object made in an earlier period'. Collecting antiques has become so popular these days that all sorts of things that a few years ago just wouldn't have been saleable are now fetching respectable sums.

A quiz book that also gives useful information will help you become more knowledgeable about antiques – far better than reading reams of dry copy. And there is a competition for readers to enter, with attractive prizes for the winners.

Bring the past alive

What people so often forget about antiques is that they are, for the most part, about *people* in the past. They're the things they used on a day-to-day basis: the things they decorated their houses with, the things they looked at, played with, ate with, beautified themselves with, worked with, cooked with and read. And it's because of this that antique goods are one of the richest sources of social history. They furnish the type of detail that brings the past and its people alive.

The human factor, of course, has been one of the reasons why the BBC *Antiques Roadshow* has always been so popular. It's fascinating to see people take along the beautiful, the workaday, the mundane and the downright curious to an expert and watch him or her recognise it for what it is, what it does or did, how it works or worked – and how much it's worth now. Whole new worlds can suddenly open up given this bit

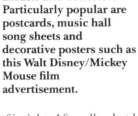

Ephemera of all kinds attracts avid collectors. Particularly popular are postcards, music hall song sheets and decorative posters such as this Walt Disney/Mickey Mouse film advertisement.

of insight. After all, what kind of society is it that has a need for button-hooks, glove stretchers or shaving books?

The big salerooms, Christies, Sotheby's and Phillips, all do their own roadshows when groups of saleroom experts travel to a particular destination where the general public have been invited to bring their objects for appraisal and valuation.

Sometimes there are quizzes as well, with prizes given by the firms themselves. Those who have consulted the experts aren't asked to sell – but if they want to, then arrangements are made to put their pieces in a suitable sale.

What is often the fascination of these sessions is the value some pieces can realise when the owners had only thought them of curiosity value – like the Ming jar that had been used for years to serve the dog's food, or the old violin found discarded in an attic that fetched thousands of pounds. Such stories as these are good PR for the salerooms and they're quick at using them as publicity; but it's true enough that such finds and

windfalls can happen, and is enough to fire the public's interest in antiques. After all, nearly everyone has old heirlooms, a junk room or attic, and who knows what treasures could be hidden therein? You might be able to spot something valuable yourself with this book as a guide.

It's often surprising with antiques to discover what is valuable and what isn't. That vase that aunty loved and cherished for years might turn out to be worthless after all, while the Mickey Mouse memorabilia left in the toy-box, forgotten for years, could well realise riches.

This book, besides testing your knowledge, will also point out different characteristics in antiques, will show you how to recognise pieces, how to classify them and how to spot those minute, but all-important differences between a thing that's valuable in the monetary sense and one that should only be prized for its looks or sentimental value.

In this way you'll soon find you're well on the way to acquiring quite a lot of knowledge in the field

– all valuable and essential when it comes to buying, collecting and selling antiques, which is something that more and more people these days are doing.

The Lure of Antiques

What's the attraction of collecting antiques? We've already touched on the knowledge of social history they can give you – and just gleaning those interesting titbits might be enough for you. And we've talked too about the excitement of gaining a windfall. But why else do people get so involved with antiques – even give up safe careers sometimes to take it up on a professional level? Not only is it a fascinating hobby, but it's one with which you can furnish your house in an individual way, and even make money, if your commercial sense is good enough.

Let's suppose you want to buy antiques and start to build up a collection. What should the beginner – or relative beginner – start with? Well, first of all, you should only buy the things you like. That might sound obvious enough, but it's surprising how many people can end up buying something they felt was in 'good taste' – even it that taste isn't theirs.

If you feel you haven't developed a definite taste yet, then go to salerooms, read books, browse around shops and even visit museums until different periods and types of merchandise become familiar, and you can say with conviction what you really do and don't like.

Too many of us dislike simply what we're unfamiliar with, or what we were brought up to think of as old-fashioned. For instance, lots of us used to hate the heaviness and ornateness of Victorian antiques – but once they became more familiar and we got accustomed to their scale and style, they became once more completely acceptable. And it's still fairly common – particularly among people of 50 plus – to dislike thirties' pieces – quite simply because that's what was around when they were young and now they associate them with depression times, and having to make do with 'old' and secondhand things when they started to set up as young adults. But now a whole new generation is recognising the intrinsic beauty of Art Deco and is prepared to part with substantial amounts of money for it.

Beware, too, of buying something simply because you were told it would be a good investment. Antiques generally *are* good investments (more about that below), but at this stage anything you buy simply has to please you. After all, you're going to have to live with it. And you don't want to have to live in a curio shop, do you?

Most of the pieces you buy will probably be used for decorating or furnishing your home. And as everyone has to have furniture, crockery, carpets, etc, you'd be spending that money anyway, buying or replacing goods. And if these things are antique, then you can be sure your home will be both interesting and different from the run-of-the-mill, chain-store-furnished variety – and not necessarily at any extra cost. It will take more time to set up, but it will also be more fun.

Furnishing an old house is also easier if you do it in the authentic furniture of the period. Thus a Victorian terraced house is marvellous done up with Victoriana, an eighteenth-century cottage is truly enticing decorated with country-style pieces of the same era, and a thirties' flat is lovely filled with Art Deco pieces. Study old pictures and photographs to get the feel of the

A very decorative English silver gilt and hardstone casket (4½″ wide) which has a moulded cagework mount decorated with cast scrolls, flowers and other motifs above openwork panel supports enriched with putti. It was made in 1847 and sold in 1984 for £1265.

time and to distil the essence of how they used to put places together – the way you arrange things can make all the difference to authenticity.

Of course, you don't have to stick rigidly to the period of your house when decorating. You can use old pieces in almost any house if you choose carefully and don't try to put in things that just aren't right: are too big and massive, for instance, or too dark and sombre so they end up overpowering the place. And filling a new and soulless house with old pieces is the quickest and easiest way of giving it a heart – and a sense of instant history.

Neither do you have to limit yourself to just one period when collecting. Putting together a free-range mix of different eras can create something quite special and very individual – but you have to have a finely honed aesthetic sense to do it right. And if you have, then really the only thing that's needed to pull a look together is that each piece has the link of your own taste. Get it right and you can give a whole new meaning to the term 'eclectic'.

Of course, you might not want to furnish your house in antiques, but might wish simply to have a collection or two. Keys, irons, corkscrews, gloves, shoe-trees, cups, postcards, teapots, old bottles – the list is endless of the things you can collect. It's up to you to choose the thing you want and to go about finding the objects. You'll find it will provide you with an irresistible hobby, and every antique shop, market or sale and every new town or village will be a trove of potential treasures for you. You'll also find no one will be stuck for what to buy you when it comes to choosing presents.

How you display a collection can either make or break the impact it has, so think about it carefully. The setting and the method you choose has to go with both the objects themselves, and the room it's in. Keys look good in the kitchen on a simple board of white, studded with nails to hold them. That way, the pretty outlines of the keys can be seen to best advantage and they gain from being confined to a limited space – simply because they're fairly small in themselves. On the other hand, plates look better when spaced out and can form an almost unlimited display. Leading from the entrance hall and

disappearing up the stairs, say, can look enticing, and witty. And hats look fantastic on a hat-stand specially bought for the purpose – as if you have inside the sitting-room a selection of visitors from Victorian, Edwardian, twenties, forties and fifties eras.

But more important than all this is the consideration of how much money you've got to spend, and how much space you've got to give. Don't set yourself the ambition of buying rare porcelain if it's going to break the bank. And if your house is crowded already, collecting apostle spoons is going to be better for your home life than stuffed animals. It's usually always a good idea to follow any special interests you might already have. That way, you can become an expert on a certain subject eventually. For instance, if you're fascinated by rock and roll, or a particular artiste in that era, or by a certain film star, then develop your interest – and collect all the memorabilia you can. And if certain gadgets or pieces of fairly esoteric equipment hold a fatal fascination for you – then follow it. Buy everything related to your subject that you can, and really learn about it. Don't forget that new areas of interest are always being opened up. After all, who would have thought second-hand kitsch would ever have a market?

The Investment factor
The antiques market is known to be a volatile one, depending very much for its rise and falls on money

This fine Canton famille rose punch bowl is approximately two feet in diameter. It is elaborately printed with dignitaries, court ladies, actors and attendants with a rim frieze of butterflies, peonies, fruit and birds on gilt ground. Made in the early 19th century, it has had a half-inch chip in the rim restored and is worth from £3000 to £5000.

markets, currency rates, the changes in public taste and even political stability. For instance, unrest in the Middle East can easily cut demand for certain types of antiques that usually sell very well in those countries.

Yet, on the whole, antiques do represent a fairly stable and good investment. Why? Because they are rare and becoming rarer by definition. Their numbers can't increase, yet they can get broken or spoilt. They usually represent good-quality workmanship and materials of the sort that are becoming rare now, simply because of economics. New pieces become second-hand if they're resold, but antiques simply become older and rarer.

Having decided which areas really interest you, the next step is buying. And in no other field is buying and selling quite so dependent on the personality of the people involved – on both sides of the fence. There are some fascinating characters in the antiques trade – and this is where you find that out for yourself. Antiques is a game open to all comers, with completely different spending powers and completely different levels of knowledge.

The interesting thing about the world of antiques, and what makes it fascinating to buyer and seller alike, is that everything in it has an individual quality. If you're dealing with handmade pieces, you have to expect some differences, and when you're dealing with old things, you have to expect different conditions.

It's possible, of course, to give general price guides that give an indication of what's happening in the overall market in a particular year, but each individual sale is unique.

The price paid depends very much on the sharp-wittedness of the buyer – and what the seller will ultimately let the piece go for.

How to Buy

Buying from a shop is probably the easiest way for the dabbler to start. And, once again, you'll find a whole range of shops to choose from. There's the junk or curio shop, ideal

Not many homes have room for a suit of armour such as this one. The helmet was made in Italy, the breastplate in Germany, the backplate in Brunswick. Not having been made by a single armourer, it is known as a composite armour. 16th century, worth about £14000.

for browsing and offering plenty of opportunities for picking up the odd bargain and strange piece – particularly in out-of-the-way country places.

But don't be lulled into thinking that *anything* bought in odd corners of the country is bound to represent good value. Many Welsh villages, for instance, are visited so regularly by professional dealers, the owners can hardly be accused of innocence and naivety when it comes to market values.

Then there are the more up-market shops in towns and country areas alike who probably rely for much of their business on the trade and export market, but who are always in business for private customers.

You might well find they have a code, rather than a price written out in pounds and pence on their goods. This usually represents a target price for the private buyer, and a trade price for a fellow dealer, which allows him or her to make a profit when selling on.

Each shop has its own secret code, usually with letters to represent each figure 1 to 0. Suppose the key to a code in one shop is A BROWN SUIT. If the shop-owner has a piece whose target price is £350, then it will be marked RWT/RTT.

It's quite easy, therefore, particularly if you ask one or two prices to check, to work out that a two-figure code represents up to £99, three is in the hundreds, and four is in the thousands – and so on. Knowing that will stop you wasting both your time and the dealer's time in asking the price of things way beyond your purse. Dealers aren't renowned for a kind and understanding attitude to people who waste their time and seem to be treating their shop as a place of general interest rather than business.

It is possible to bargain in a shop. Ask the dealer if that's the best price he can do. He may come down, he may not. Bringing a wad of cash can often be a fine incentive too – the sight of cash and the prospect of a quick deal always being attractive – but don't push beyond that. A dealer won't sell if 'there's nothing in it for him' – i.e. he won't be making a profit – unless he fears he won't be able to sell the piece at all and he wants to recoup some stock money. If you do try to go beyond his limits, a dealer may well refuse to trade with you.

Ask too in a shop if VAT is included in the quoted price. You'll have to add it on at the current rate, so take that into account in your financial calculations.

And remember that if you've pretended to be trade in order to get a low price when bargaining, you may well have forfeited your legal protection as a customer. Transactions at that stage are very much a question of buying 'as seen' – so buyer beware! You must be pretty sure of what you're looking at.

The upper end of the market where the finest pieces are sold at frighteningly high prices is usually for the connoisseur, and the richest and most knowledgeable of trade – so this doesn't really concern us here.

For some time, the antiques trade took little notice of Edwardian furniture because it had not achieved sufficient age to merit the title 'antique'. Nevertheless, there were many superbly made pieces produced during the early years of this century, often finely veneered and inlaid – as this mahogany and marquetry cylinder bureau shows. Its value is between £2500 and £3500.

Markets

Local markets are another good source of finds of antiques and junk. And they're great fun as well. There are several in London: Portobello Road, Camden Passage, Brick Lane etc – ring up the relevant local council to find out when they're on.

And many country towns and villages have good markets. They're usually advertised, by poster or in the local paper, but it's often worthwhile asking a local dealer when and where they're held. Here, it's very much a question of pot luck as to what's available on any particular day, and it's a good idea to go as early as possible. That's how you'll beat the dealers and get the best bargains.

Bargaining in a market is half the fun of being there, and it might be worthwhile sharpening up your business transactions with a few tricks of the trade. Remember you'll get more discount the more you buy in one go. So if you're tempted by three or four things on one stall, put them together and offer your price for cash for the job lot. You can also ask certain dealers if they have any more of the same sort of thing if you're looking to build up a special collection – that way, they'll be on the look-out in their working travels to find things they know they have a customer for.

Auctions and salerooms

But it's auctions at salerooms that can really represent the most fun, once you've acquired a working amount of knowledge. There are four big London salerooms: Christies, Sotheby's, Phillips, and Bonhams, who have regular types of different auctions. Write to them for information about the forthcoming sales you think might interest you.

And as well as the major London salerooms, there are plenty of country salerooms that generally advertise in the local papers when a sale is due.

You'll find that buying in this way is fun, gets the adrenalin going and – once you've had a few of your bids romp home – becomes a taste you can develop quite an addiction for.

Auctions are often frequented by dealers looking for stock. Don't be frightened to bid against them: an auction is open to all. Usually it's every man for himself at an auction. In fact, when you are bidding against dealers, it's a sign the piece is both desirable and, up until the minute he drops out, a good bargain, likely to make an immediate profit. This is because he's probably buying for a shop and he has a good idea of what he can get for something – but he wants his profit margin too: so if the bidding starts to edge into that area, he'll

A fine set of three Regency parcel gilt and ebonised open armchairs was exhibited at the Royal Pavilion, Brighton. This was one of them, photographed for an auction catalogue in 1984.

probably back out. Even if you carry on a bit beyond that, you'll still be buying for less than you would have to pay in a shop in all probability.

Being at an auction for the first time can be fairly intimidating, nevertheless, so let's get a few things straight. Involuntary gestures like rubbing your nose or winking aren't usually mistaken for a bid on your part, that lands you with something you neither want nor can afford. Auctioneers develop a sixth sense about who's bidding

and who isn't – and if there is any doubt they'll usually stop to make sure before continuing.

Nevertheless, it is true that such gestures as these do represent methods of bidding for some people – but these are usually regular customers who know the auctioneer. In some sales, for instance, a man will be bidding when his last waistcoat button is undone, and will have finished when it's buttoned up. It's all this sort of thing, though, that contributes to the unique and

exciting atmosphere that can be found at the big salerooms when an important sale is in action. The bidders compete secretively, often represented by a deputy; the seller, if present, will eagerly wait for the reserve price to be reached, then passed. And behind it all, orchestrating the whole game, is the calm and highly trained auctioneer, moving bids upwards by tens, hundreds or even thousands of pounds at a time. Then suddenly the limit of the contenders is reached, one person's tenacity repays him or her and with one tap from the gavel it's all over, and a piece of worth and beauty changes hands, once again.

Auctioneers, however, do like clients and customers to be familiar with the drill, so it pays to know who's who, and what's what, and it's much the same at any auction, whether highly prestigious or comparatively humble. An auctioneer doesn't buy himself – he is simply an agent with the brief to obtain the highest price possible for the seller. Then he takes his commission from that. Sometimes buyers are charged a premium. So if you're buying, you must check the saleroom's rules and conditions carefully. Look in the catalogue of each sale to find them.

It's essential you set yourself a personal limit for each piece you're interested in buying. Work it out and write it in the margin beside the number of each potential purchase. And don't forget to add on the buyer's premiums if there is one, as well as VAT. It's up to you then to examine carefully whatever you might buy during viewing hours,

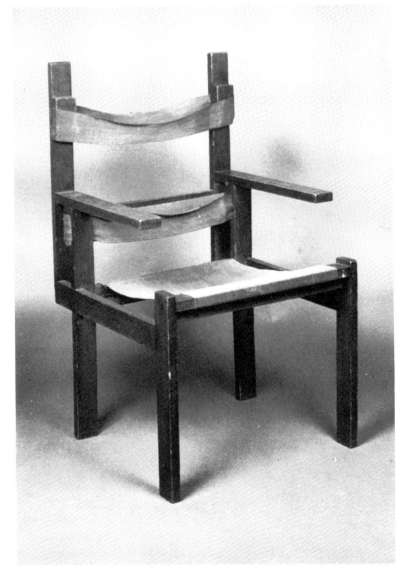

In stark contrast to the decorative elegance of the Regency chair opposite, this is an oak lath armchair, made almost exactly a century later. It was designed by Marcel Breuer for the famous Bauhaus and attracted a price of £21000 at a 1985 auction.

which are usually on the morning of the sale or the day before.

Get to the sale in good time because you've got no way of knowing just how quickly each sale might be dispatched with. When you want to bid, make a definite sign: raise your hand or your catalogue, for instance. After that, you have to bid again every time someone else has outbid you. Don't go over the limit you set yourself in the heat of the moment. If you want to stop bidding, shake your head next time the auctioneer looks at you. If you do buy, make sure you can arrange for transport fairly quickly – you'll be expected to remove your purchase pretty speedily, or pay for storage.

And once you've got your purchases home, then you must remember one of the most important factors of being a collector. And that's care. Every piece you collect – because it is old and rare or comparatively rare –

must be looked after carefully both to look as good as possible now and give you maximum pleasure, and to last for the future.

Whether it's an old pine chest, a Chippendale chair, a porcelain vase, a packet of old postcards, Dinky toys, dolls or silver candlesticks – all can lose their beauty and worth by clumsy handling and exposure to pests that attack them and pollutants that ruin them.

Modern air-conditioning and central heating are not good for papers, leather and woods. So don't set them too high and don't turn them on in the autumn if they're not really needed. Make sure the humidity level is right in the room – around 60 per cent is about right (a small instrument called a hygrometer will keep check). At too high a level the damp atmosphere will encourage fungus and moulds. Too dry, and leather, paper and wood will dry out.

Pests, such as woodworm and moths, should be watched for. Banish them with proprietary products designed for the purpose which can be bought from local hardware stores.

Wash china and glass one piece at a time, go easy on the detergent and make sure it's all rinsed off. And always make sure picture and plate hangings are *very* secure.

As you become more and more familiar with antiques and the ways of the antique world, you'll find your knowledge growing – and with it your pleasure. If this book inspires you to take up antiques as a hobby, if it proves to you how fascinating a subject antiques are, and if it teaches you something about them, then it's succeeded. You might feel inspired with your new-found knowledge to enter the competition (page 147). There are £5000 worth of prizes to be won, and the competition is open until 1 November 1986. **Martin Miller**

It was Sheraton who designed the first sofa table. Its length, he said, should be five feet six inches with the flaps raised, the width two feet, and the height two feet four inches. This early 19th-century Continental example is of mahogany crossbanded with satinwood, and is some eight inches shorter than Sheraton would have liked. Nevertheless, today's trend is towards smaller furniture, and this one would command around £2500 at auction.

A fine Japanese carved ivory group of two actors, each
wearing a mask and carrying a short sword, incised
overall with brown-stained intricate detail. It is just over
6½ inches high and was made in the late 19th century.
Pieces like this hold their value – this one realised £1450
in 1983.

Beds

It would seem that, wherever civilisation arose, the bed appeared as one of its earliest manifestations. Thus it is that we find Tutankhamun's grandparents to have been possessed of a bedstead 3500 years ago. Nevertheless, it was not until medieval times that the British concerned themselves with such symbols of status and wealth.

The large beds of the wealthy, roofed over and draped all round, formed almost, when closed, a room within a room – and the 'close' beds of the Scots, with wooden doors, might best be described as sleeping cupboards. In the days when night air was considered to bring sickness and, to the superstitious, even worse, it is hardly surprising that such measures were taken for its exclusion.

In those early days – and in some remoter country districts even into the nineteenth century – it was not uncommon for travellers to share a bed with total strangers, though due attention was paid to rank and status when such arrangements were made. Which puts into context the famed 'Great Bed of Ware' which was reputed to have been large enough to accommodate six couples with ease.

1

What is this called:
1) a chaise longue 2) a sleeping chair
3) a day bed 4) a couch

2

What period is it:
1) late C.15th 2) early C.17th
3) late C.17th 4) mid C.18th

3

What is the 'roof' of a four-poster bed called:
1) tester 2) canopy 3) cornice
4) 1 and 2

4

One of these four-poster beds is C.17th, the other a C.19th interpretation – which is which?

5

What is this type of bed called:
1) low 2) truckle 3) valet
4) pallet

Who used it:
a) servants b) mistresses
c) children d) the elderly

6

This French bed is called a:
1) lit abattant 2) lit couchant
3) lit polonais 4) lit littoral

7

It can also be called a:
1) half tester 2) pulpit bed
3) duchess bed

8

This bed is English but is
strongly influenced by which
foreign style:
1) Shaker 2) Empire 3) rococo
4) Egyptian

9

This C.19th pine bed is called
a:
1) folding 2) truckle
3) spare 4) cupboard
bed

19

Bookcases

As everyone knows, it was William Caxton who introduced movable-type printing into Britain in 1477 with his *Dictes or Sayengis of the Philosophres*. Nevertheless, it was some two centuries before domestic bookcases found their way into use. The masculine lines of early bookcases are testament to the fact that the library was a male preserve where a gentleman could browse over his folios, read the classical authors, consult the terrestrial or celestial globes or read the latest novel in broad-sheet, away from female chatter.

It was not long before the (quite logical) combination of a bookcase with a bureau became fashionable. The practicality of these, and the later secretaire bookcases, ensured not only their continued manufacture but also the well-preserved survival of early examples.

Until quite recently, good but large eighteenth-century bookcases were relatively cheap. However, the quality of construction and fine materials are now being increasingly appreciated – and even the largest examples are becoming increasingly expensive.

1
What is the correct description:
1) *a kneehole bureau bookcase*
2) *a kneehole bureau bookcase cabinet*
3) *a bureau bookcase*

3
Why is this bookcase called a breakfront:
1) *because it has four doors*
2) *because the central section stands out from the rest*
3) *because the cornice is dentilled*

2
Which famous diarist had this oak bookcase specially made for him *c*.1666:
1) *Samuel Pepys* 2) *Bishop Burnet*
3) *John Evelyn*

4
What is the central flap-down drawer called:
1) *a tambour* 2) *a slide drawer*
3) *a secretaire* 4) *a fall-front drawer*

5
What are the strips of wood dividing up the glass on the doors called:
1) *glazing bars* 2) *fillets*
3) *astragals* 4) *1 and 3*

6

What period is this piece of furniture:
1) *Charles II* 2) *George III*
3) *Victorian* 4) *Edwardian*

7

The most popular wood for furniture of this time was:
1) *oak* 2) *walnut*
3) *mahogany* 4) *satinwood*

8

In what year did Chippendale first publish his book 'The Gentleman and Cabinet Maker's Director':
1) *1745* 2) *1754* 3) *1767* 4) *1771*

9

Is the correct name for the decoration on the top of this bookcase:
1) *volutes* 2) *broken pediment*
3) *swan-necked pediment*
4) *ovolo cornice*

10

Is the top of this piece decorated with:
1) *a gap-tooth pediment*
2) *a broken pediment*
3) *a classical cresting*
4) *an oeil de boeuf*

11

This mahogany secretaire bookcase is of which period:
1) *George III* 2) *William IV*
3) *Regency* 4) *Empire*

Bureaux

It is generally accepted that, somewhere in the medieval melting pot, bible boxes developed into writing slopes hinged at the back like old-fashioned school desk tops. Later, the hinges were moved to the front, which allowed the sloping lid to fall forward onto supports providing a flat surface for writing with storage space behind. Divide the storage space with pigeonholes and drawers and build it onto a stand also equipped with drawers – and the bureau adopts the form that has remained since the latter years of the seventeenth century. The actual word 'bureau' has an equally convoluted derivation. It begins with the Latin 'burrus', russet red, which was the colour of the dye used in the manufacture of a coarse cloth, 'bure', used on the Continent by clerks in the Middle Ages to protect writing surfaces. This developed into the French 'bureau' or office – and what is the piece of furniture but a small office?

Naturally enough, furniture designers over the years found other ways of combining writing surfaces with storage compartments for both domestic and commercial use, which accounts for the splendid variety of furniture made for this single purpose. Not least of the pleasures of desks and bureaux are the secret compartments and concealed catches which most contain.

1

When the front of a desk like this is opened, the inside is revealed fitted with:
1) cupboards 2) pigeonholes
3) filing holes 4) small drawers

2

This type of desk is called:
1) kneehole 2) secretaire
3) flat-top 4) agent's

3

This desk, with drawers to front and back, is known as:
1) library 2) rent 3) partners'
4) architect's

4

This type of Louis XIV desk is called a:
1) bureau de jour
2) bureau Richelieu
3) bureau Mazarin

5

It is decorated with a type of brass and tortoiseshell inlay known as:
1) Boulle 2) arabesques
3) vernis Martin 4) scagliola

6

This is called:
1) a Somerset House
2) an Apsley House
3) a Buckingham House
4) a Carlton House
writing table

7

This type of small C.19th desk is termed a:
1) Devonport 2) Davenport
3) military desk 4) Gladstone desk

8

This little desk is:
1) English 2) German
3) French 4) Italian

9

It is known as:
1) a bonheur du jour
2) an escritoire
3) a Croft 4) a secretary

10

This rosewood marquetry cylinder bureau dates from *c*.1870. Is its style:
1) Dutch 2) French
3) German 4) English

11

The opening top of this desk is known as:
1) the closer 2) the rods
3) the tambour 4) the cresta

a

12

Match the description to the illustration:
1) a Queen Anne walnut bureau
2) an Edwardian mahogany veneered bureau
3) a Queen Anne walnut bureau-on-stand
4) a George I walnut bureau

b

c

d

Cabinets

Political and culinary connotations aside, cabinets might best be described as lockable cupboards intended for the storage and display of rare or treasured possessions. What sets a cabinet apart from a cupboard as a piece of furniture is the degree of craftsmanship and the quality of materials used in its manufacture.

The subtleties of civilised living were much slower to be accepted in Britain than in many Continental countries, and virtually all refinements of taste and manners were imported from France, Italy and Holland. Where wealthy Continentals would display their status by means of possessions of exquisite delicacy and craftsmanship, the British were far more likely to simply heap a crudely made cupboard with pewter or silver and leave it at that. However, during the seventeenth century, when Continental influences began to make themselves felt, there began to be a demand for the finer things of life. Sadly, British standards of craftsmanship were not up to the job, and cabinet-makers were encouraged to leave home and set up shop in Britain. Thus, all our early cabinets either display marked European characteristics, or were imported from the Far East.

The lacquer work of the Oriental imports began such a fashion that, by the late seventeenth century, young ladies of genteel birth were actually attending classes to learn the art of do-it-yourself lacquer work. The results never came near to matching the original.

During the eighteenth and nineteenth centuries, as the English Gentleman developed a taste for learning, there was a 'cabinet explosion' with pieces custom made for the storage and display of everything from archaeological finds to butterflies and birds' eggs. Many of these are unquestionably English in style and manufacture, and rank among the finest of all English antique furniture.

a

b

c

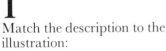

d

1

Match the description to the illustration:

1) *a Queen Anne lacquer cabinet-on-chest*
2) *a George I walnut secretaire cabinet*
3) *a Sheraton satinwood dressing cabinet c.1795*
4) *an Art Nouveau mahogany display cabinet c.1900*

2

The panels on this late C.17th
cabinet-on-stand are:
1) painted 2) carved
3) inlaid 4) japanned

3

What period is this cabinet:
1) Queen Anne 2) George II
3) Regency 4) Victorian

4

In what style is this cabinet:
1) Art Nouveau 2) Modernist
3) Gothic Revival 4) Art Deco

5

This type of cabinet-on-stand
fitted with series of slim drawers
was often used to store
collections of:
1) intaglios 2) cameos 3) medals
4) coins 5) all of these

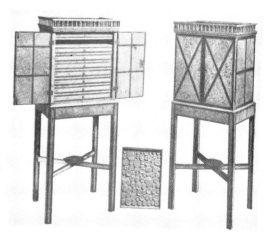

7

This cabinet desk is an example of which style:
1) *Rococo* 2) *Anglo-Indian*
3) *Chinoiserie* 4) *neo-classical*

6

The geometric pattern on the doors of this cabinet is achieved by a method of inlaying thin strips of wood called:
1) *marquetry* 2) *jigsaw pattern*
3) *parquetry*
4) *parquet de Versailles*

The drawer is decorated with a pattern known as:
a) *filigree* b) *guilloche*
c) *Chinese diamond*
d) *blind fretwork*

8

This cabinet was made in the style of which designer:
1) *Gillows* 2) *Adam*
3) *Seddon* 4) *Hepplewhite*

9

This cabinet is decorated in a technique fashionable in the:
1) *Carolean* 2) *Regency*
3) *Victorian*
period called:
a) *pen-work* b) *Etruscan*
c) *vernis Martin* d) *grisaille*

10

This display cabinet would have been placed:
1) *between two windows*
2) *in an alcove* 3) *in a corner*
4) *in a stair-well*

11

This cabinet is in which style:
1) *Rococo Revival*
2) *'Chinese Chippendale'*
3) *Gothic Revival*
4) *Liberty style*

12

This type of mid-Victorian cabinet, with mirrored back, is sometimes called a:
1) *credenza* 2) *sideboard*
3) *buffet* 4) *toilette*

14

Is this cabinet:
1) *Dutch* 2) *Anglo-Dutch*
3) *Chinese* 4) *Japanese*

13

This:
1) *German* 2) *Dutch*
3) *Scandinavian*
display cabinet is decorated in:
a) *seaweed marquetry*
b) *oyster marquetry*
c) *floral marquetry*
d) *scroll marquetry*

Chests

The very first chests were merely hollowed-out sections of tree trunk with crudely fitting lids, used for storage and safekeeping of valuables. These 'trunks' were used, too, as collection boxes in churches when funds were required to finance the Crusades. Eventually, the hollowed-out tree trunk was superseded by the boarded chest which could be made to any size and which was less subject to splitting. These chests originally consisted of six thick boards pegged together but, as the craft developed, it was found that stronger and lighter pieces could be made by constructing joined frames grooved to take panels. The corner stiles, extended below the chest to form legs, raised it off the ground to reduce the damage caused by damp earth and stone floors.

Early chests served a multitude of purposes, from storage to seating to workbench – even to sleeping. The inclusion of drawers made access to stored belongings easier, and the addition of raised backs and sides saw the birth of the settle.

1

This trunk is made from timber with a distinctive odour. It is:
1) *rosewood* 2) *camphorwood*
3) *tulipwood* 4) *fruitwood*

2

What date is this chest:
1) *c.1300* 2) *c.1500* 3) *c.1800*

3

Would the decorations on this chest be termed:
1) *Gothic* 2) *Celtic* 3) *gothick*
4) *mannerist*

4

This type of Italian Renaissance chest is called a:
1) *canzone* 2) *carmeloin*
3) *cassone* 4) *credenza*

5

The type of panelling on this chest is called:
1) *flamiform* 2) *linenfold*
3) *drapery* 4) *pleated*

6

This early chest is most likely to be made of:
1) *walnut* 2) *ash* 3) *beech* 4) *oak*

Chairs

Our earliest general-use chairs are 'wainscot' chairs. These developed from seats built into the wainscot panelling of noble houses. Early chairs were often covered in velvet or leather, and rare seventeenth-century examples can still be seen at Knole, Sevenoaks.

During the eighteenth century, the form and outline of the chair became increasingly sophisticated as oak and beech gave way to walnut and, later, mahogany. At this time, chairs were often made en suite with settees and ranged around the walls of domestic reception rooms, only being drawn up to table or fireside when they were required for use.

Easy chairs as we know them did not appear on the scene until after 1828, in which year one Samuel Pratt patented his circular wire coiled springs for deep sprung upholstery.

1 Match type of leg or foot to illustration:
1) claw and ball foot
2) scroll foot 3) lion's paw foot
4) cabriole leg 5) pad foot
6) spade foot 7) blind fret
8) sabre leg

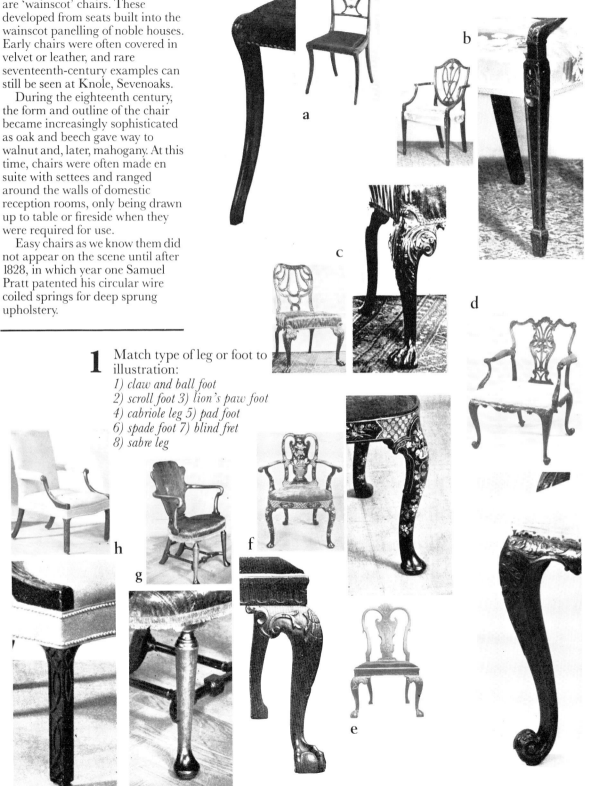

2

This chair is decorated in a technique called:
1) mercury gilding 2) blind gilding
3) water gilding 4) gilt marquetting

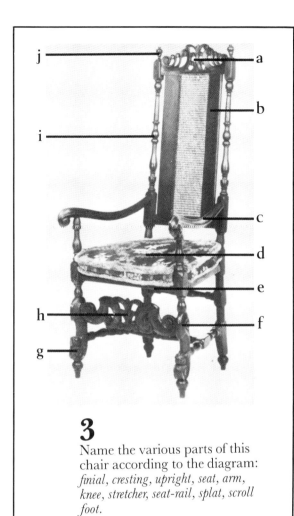

3

Name the various parts of this chair according to the diagram:
finial, cresting, upright, seat, arm, knee, stretcher, seat-rail, splat, scroll foot.

4

Is this chair in the style of:
1) Queen Anne 2) George I
3) George II 4) George III

5

What period is this chair:
1) George III 2) Regency
3) Victorian 4) Edwardian

a

b

c

d

e

f

g

h

i

j

6

Match the description to the illustration:
1) tub 2) fiddle-back 3) ladder-back
4) Chinese fretwork 5) winged
6) thrown 7) cane 8) shell
9) interlaced 10) rococo

7

These chairs are all:
1) carvers 2) porter's 3) hall
4) collapsible

8

Where would you find this type
of chair:
1) chapel 2) kitchen 3) lounge
4) library

9

Is this known as a:
1) chaise longue 2) chaise courte
3) chaise duchesse 4) lit au cheval

It can be converted into:
a) a prie-dieu b) a table
c) a pair of steps d) a lounger

10

The type of painting on this
C.18th/19th chair was heavily
influenced by the excavation of
which city:
1) Delphi 2) Pompeii 3) Rome
4) Halicarnassus

11

When was this chair designed:
1) c.1800 2) c.1907 3) c.1920
4) c.1950

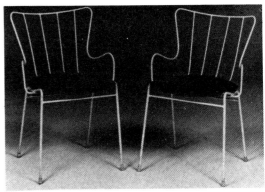

12

These chairs were designed for which occasion:
1) *Monza Exhibition 1930*
2) *Exposition Universelle, Brussels 1958*
3) *Great Exhibition 1851*
4) *Festival of Britain 1951/52*

13

This type of chair of the end quarter C.18th is sometimes called a:
1) *corner* 2) *Windsor* 3) *Derbyshire*
4) *banister back*
chair

14

What was this Welsh country pine chair traditionally known for:
1) *sleeping* 2) *lambing*
3) *nursing* 4) *carrying*

15

This is called a:
1) *gambling* 2) *lounging*
3) *'horse'* 4) *cockfighting*
chair

16

Is this called a:
1) *master's* 2) *chairman's*
3) *president's* 4) *governor's*
chair

17

Windsor chairs were most often made of elm and beech. More desirable examples were partly or wholly of:
1) yew 2) holly
3) bog oak 4) pear wood

18

Elegant chairs such as these, painted and part gilded, are typical of which period:
1) William IV 2) Regency
3) mid-Victorian 4) Edwardian

19

This sturdy and inexpensive chair is known as a:
1) fiddler's arch
2) potman's bender
3) smoker's bow
4) barber's horseshoe

20

Very finely made furniture of simple 'country' design suggests which country of origin:
1) America 2) Holland
3) China 4) Denmark

21

This low chair has a characteristically long seat and well-padded back. It is known as:
1) a nursing chair
2) an invalid seat
3) a bustle chair
4) a long Liza

Settees, Sofas & Couches

Nowadays, the words sofa and settee are more or less interchangeable. Originally, a settee was made for two or more people to sit on in modest comfort, whereas a sofa was more of a lounging piece of furniture. Both may be said to be descended from the settle, though the relative luxury of the sofa has Eastern connotations.

The settle is a direct descendant of the chest, made all of wood, with a vertical back onto which is sometimes built a cupboard. Few settees were made until after the Restoration, and then were influenced by chair design, with which they were often made en suite. Consequently, they tend to have a lightness and elegance which, to some extent, compensates for their lack of comfort.

The natural extension of the sofa is, of course, the chesterfield; large, fat and overstuffed and sometimes extremely comfortable.

But perhaps the most comfortable of all, and certainly the most romantic, is the chaise longue. This is a development of the day bed, having an extended arm along one side and, often, some fine carving on the exposed wooden frame.

1

What is this type of seat called:
1) a bench 2) a sofa 3) a settle
4) a box bench

2

Label these sofas correctly:
1) Louis XV walnut sofa
2) Louis XVI giltwood sofa
3) Regency rosewood sofa
4) American mahogany sofa c.1850

a

b

c

d

3

Where would this bench have been placed, in the:
1) hall 2) conservatory
3) chapel 4) dining room

4

Who was this bench made for:
1) dogs 2) chickens 3) children

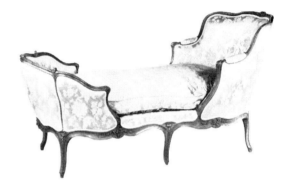

5

This type of 'lounger' is termed:
1) a boat sofa 2) a two-ended chair
3) a duchesse en bateau
4) a duchesse brisée

6

What is this settee made from:
1) cast iron 2) papier mâché
3) thatch 4) wicker

7

What is the popular name for this settee:
1) love seat 2) pouffe
3) 'S' settee 4) conversation settee

Chests of Drawers & Commodes

Sometime during the mid-sixteenth century, European craftsmen began to make lidded chests with one or two rows of drawers in the bottom. It is easy to see why these revolutionised domestic storage, particularly of clothes made of fine, easily creased fabrics. Then as now, the English were quick to adopt stylish innovation from the Continent, and mule chests, as these are called, became very popular.

In view of this it is perhaps surprising that the fully-fledged chest of drawers seems to have taken almost a further hundred years to emerge. Once the practice of turning the entire chest over to drawers caught on, the storage chest as such died almost completely as far as fashion went. Poorer people, servants and conservative country folk, however, continued to use and make chests. These were generally of oak or pine.

Often kept in public or semi-public rooms, many chests of drawers were exquisitely decorated – particularly those made on the Continent. The most exotic timbers were used either as straightforward veneers or as marquetry on these Continental 'commodes', and many were further embellished with marble tops and ormolu mounts. The French name 'commode' is also used in English for a chest of drawers of French pattern.

a

b

1
Place these chests of drawers in date order:
1) mid C.17th 2) George I
3) early George III 4) early C.19th

c

d

a

b

2

Identify the basic shape of these chests from these possibilities:
1) serpentine 2) bombé
3) bow-front 4) curvilinear
5) dished 6) rectilinear
7) demi-lune

c

d

3

This piece of furniture is usually called a:
1) *chest* 2) *commode*
3) *garderobe* 4) *lowboy*

4

What is the dominant style of the decoration:
1) *rococo* 2) *baroque*
3) *neo-classical* 4) *Palladian*

5

What is the thin slide above the top drawer called:
1) *clothes slide* 2) *valet slide*
3) *brushing slide* 4) *cleaning slide*

6

Is it English or French?

a

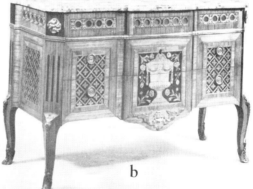

b

d

c

7

Match the description to the illustration:
1) *a Louis XV marquetry bow-fronted commode*
2) *an early Louis XV kingwood bombé commode*
3) *a Louis XV transitional commode*
4) *a Louis XVI mahogany commode*

8

This George II mahogany commode is by which famous English cabinet-maker:
1) *Thomas Chippendale*
2) *Thomas Johnson*
3) *John Linnel*
4) *William Vile*

9

Gilt-bronze mounts on this type of furniture are usually called:
1) *bronze doré* 2) *ormolu*
3) *water gilded* 4) *classical mounts*

11

The popular name for this type of chest of drawers is:
1) *spinster* 2) *bachelor*
3) *widow* 4) *bride*
chest

10

This type of chest is known in England as:
1) *a chest-on-chest* 2) *a highboy*
3) *a tallboy* 4) *1 and 3*

12

In view of their small neat appearance they are very desirable – could this one be worth between:
1) *£800-1400* 2) *£2000-3000*
3) *£5000-10000* 4) *£10000-20000*

13

What is this type of chest of drawers called:
1) *a chiffonier* 2) *a semainier*
3) *a cartonnier* 4) *a corner chest*

Cupboards & Wardrobes

As anyone who has ever visited a ruined medieval castle will know, each had a number of small, outer rooms marked on the guide book plan as 'garderobes'. These, in modern parlance, were the lavatories; austere, unhygienic and totally without plumbing. So unwholesome was the atmosphere in these rooms that no moth or mite or silverfish would ever venture in. Which, to the medieval mind, made them the ideal place in which to store the best clothes when not being worn. To guard and to ward have similar connotations, so when a piece of furniture was eventually made to take over one of the functions of the garderobe, wardrobe must have seemed as good a name for it as any.

The earliest cupboards, too, received their name from their function. They were boards upon which the family plate was displayed and stored, and took the form of fairly massive three-tiered shelf units. As time went by, they became partially – and then finally – enclosed by doors, and their use was extended to the storage of anything and everything from clothing to food to armaments.

1

This early form of cupboard is known as a Gothic:
*1) credenza 2) oriel 3) aumbry
4) hutch*

2

This C.18th Welsh cupboard is known as a:
1) tridarn 2) deudarn 3) buffet

3

Is this walnut C.17th cupboard:
*1) German 2) Flemish
3) French 4) Danish*

4

This little cupboard was designed to:
*1) fit under a bench 2) be portable
3) be dismantled 4) hang on a wall*

a

f

5

Match the illustration to the description:

1) *a Welsh oak hanging cupboard c.1670*
2) *a Louis XVI provincial oak armoire*
3) *a Dutch C.18th floral marquetry press*
4) *a George III mahogany gentleman's wardrobe*
5) *a C.18th/19th Welsh pine linen press*
6) *a 'Mouseman' oak wardrobe by Robert Thompson, 1930s*

e

c

b

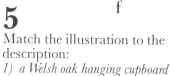

d

6

This ancestor of the modern cupboard is Jacobean and is termed a:
1) buffet 2) court cupboard
3) sideboard 4) shelf cupboard

8

The style of this cupboard is known as:
1) rococo 2) baroque
3) colonial 4) empire

9

The style developed from the neo-classical, which is often referred to as:
1) Sheraton 2) Hepplewhite
3) Adam 4) Voysey

7

You would find this cupboard in a:
1) dining room 2) hall
3) bedroom 4) library

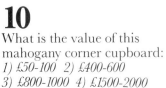

10

What is the value of this mahogany corner cupboard:
1) £50-100 2) £400-600
3) £800-1000 4) £1500-2000

11

This oak:
1) dresser 2) sideboard
3) court cupboard 4) press cupboard
dates from the:
a) early C.16th b) late C.16th
c) mid C.17th d) early C.18th

Tables

Generally speaking, a table is a table is a table. The qualities which set any one table apart from the rest are generally those of craftsmanship or specialised use. Some that combine both these qualities admirably are the eighteenth and earlier nineteenth-century games tables, often marvellously equipped for chess and backgammon, tric-trac and cribbage, with wells and drawers for storage of dice, chess and draughtsmen, cards, counters and even writing and sewing necessaries. Of all great English furniture designers, it was perhaps Sheraton who took the greatest delight in variable-purpose furniture, to the extent that he sometimes managed to endow a single piece of furniture with as many as six separate uses.

Another ingenious designer was Jupe, of Johnstone and Jupe, New Bond Street, who in 1838 patented his expanding circular table which, when wound open, separated into segments allowing as many as sixteen extra leaves to be inserted and increasing its diameter from five feet two inches to eight feet. A leaf storage cabinet was also supplied.

And then there are the gateleg tables, the drop-leaf tables – including Pembroke and Sutherland tables – the concertina tables and envelope tables; all seeking ways to overcome the age-old problem of providing extra surface area when needed without filling the room permanently with acres of polished wood.

1

The earliest form of table was probably a plank on a support called:
1) a stretcher 2) a trestle 3) an x frame
4) a joint and pole

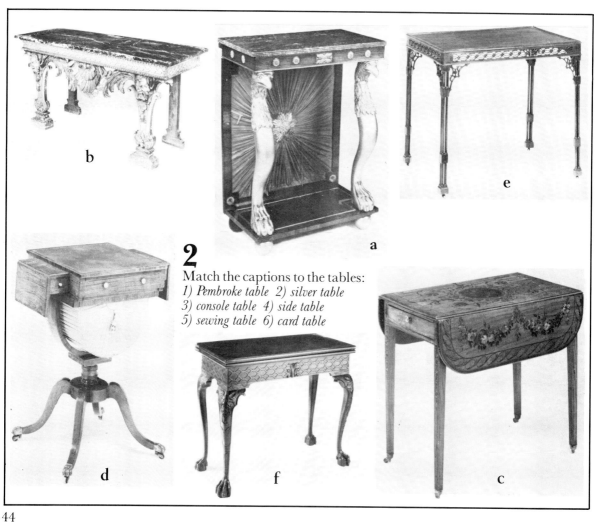

2

Match the captions to the tables:
1) Pembroke table 2) silver table
3) console table 4) side table
5) sewing table 6) card table

4

Early tables often of great length with tops made of one or more boards are called:
1) dining 2) parlour
3) dormitory 3) refectory
tables

3

This James I oak table is able to be extended by means of:
1) draw leaves at either end
2) tipping over the top
3) placing another table against it
4) using another top

5

The decoration on this side table, particularly the grotesque masks, points to which country of origin:
1) Portugal 2) Spain
3) Holland 4) Ireland

6

This side table is sometimes called a:
1) bedside table 2) lowboy
3) dummy table 4) halfboy

7

This Regency table has a hinged top. Was it designed for:
1) playing cards 2) uneven floors
3) informal breakfasts 4) reading

8

This is a Georgian:
1) gaming 2) work
3) breakfast 4) dressing
table

9

This drum table with rotating top has eight drawer fronts. How many drawers:
1) 8 2) 6 3) 4 4) 2

10

The top of this late C.18th side table is made from a composition material called:
1) barbola 2) tole 3) scagliola 4) faux marbre

11

This elaborate papier mâché work table is typically:
1) Georgian 2) William IV 3) Regency 4) Victorian

12

This is a:
1) group   of:a) quartetto
2) nest   b) work
3) compendium   c) treparto
4) nid   d) occasional
*   tables*

13

One of these is a dumb-waiter – the other is a whatnot. Which is which?

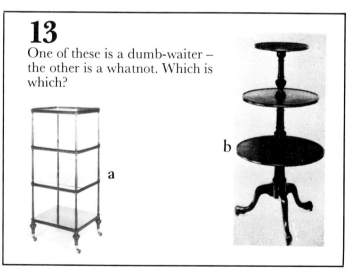

a

b

14

The top of this:
1) occasional 2) tip-top 3) tea table rests on a support called a:
a) box b) birdcage c) flywheel

15

Fit the caption to the picture:
1) *pedestal dining table*
2) *penwork games table*
3) *Victorian walnut centre table*
4) *draughtsman's kneehole table*
5) *Sheraton tricoteuse*
6) *library table* 7) *kettle stand*

a

b

c

d

e

f

g

16

How is this card table described:
1) *folding* 2) *revolving*
3) *envelope*

17

This table was used for:
1) *drawing* 2) *tea* 3) *writing*
in:
a) *Japan* b) *Malaya* c) *China*
d) *India*

Dressers & Sideboards

There existed a shelf unit in Tudor times which went by one name at the front of the house and another at the back; the shelves of Cardinal Wolsey's buffet were laden with silver to impress visitors, while his servants' dressoir (a precisely similar piece of furniture) was purely a functional aid to service at mealtimes. Such confusions sometimes still arise. We occasionally find similar pieces of furniture being described variously as dresser bases or sideboards, for example; and who can draw the line between the more delicate of bookcases and the least delicate of display cabinets? Nevertheless, the dresser, as its name implies, was originally intended for use in the dressing – or preparation – of food primarily in the kitchen, while the sideboard belonged in the dining room where it permitted final preparation and serving of food.

1

This dresser with arched cupboard beneath is sometimes called a:
1) pot dresser 2) galleried dresser
3) dog kennel dresser
4) hunter dresser

2

The upper parts of the front supports of this Regency sideboard are described as:
1) rope-twist 2) barley-sugar
3) spiral 4) barber's pole

3

Match the illustration to the description:
1) Lancashire pine dresser
2) Irish pine dresser
3) Cornish pine dresser

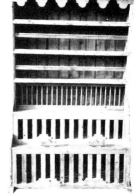

b

c

a

4

Some Irish dressers are known as:
1) plate-rack 2) chicken coop
3) fence 4) slatted
dressers

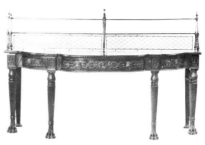

5

What period is this sideboard:
1) George II 2) William IV
3) Regency 4) Victorian

Miscellaneous Furniture

Every household function has had, at some time or other, a piece of furniture made to assist or disguise it. Although, quite often, household needs have changed, this in no way diminishes the attractiveness or interest of the redundant furniture.

Fine mahogany coalboxes are rarely used for their original purpose any more, if only because of their present cash value. Wine coolers and cellarets, three-step commodes and metamorphic library steps that convert into chairs, teapoys and butler's trays – all are quite unsuited to modern houses and modern living, but all are eminently collectable and, perhaps, even more fascinating in the glimpses they give us of earlier days.

1

What period is this stool:
1) c.1300 2) c.1560 3) c.1750
What sort of stool is it:
*a) gout b) joint c) quadruped
d) low*

2

What is this:
*1) a work-box 2) a child's chest
3) a bread trough 4) a tridarn*

3

Match the caption to the illustration:
*1) coalbox 2) bottle-stand
3) plate rack 4) wine cooler
5) cellaret 6) canterbury*

a

b

c

d

e

f

4

This Hepplewhite:
1) fire-screen 2) stick-screen
3) pole-screen 4) work-screen
was used:
a) to shield the lady's face from the fire
b) to shield the lady's face from the lamp
c) for decoration
d) to keep off draughts

5

The dish on this tazza is stamped Jennens and Bettridge. This suggests what material:
1) pewter 2) Sheffield plate
3) porcelain 4) papier mâché

6

What is this:
1) a movable trivet
2) an invalid support
3) a baby walker

7

This is a:
1) linen press 2) bachelor chest
3) trouser press 4) mangle

8

This:
1) ice bucket 2) oyster bucket
3) peat bucket 4) whitebait bucket
is:
a) Danish b) German
c) Spanish d) Irish

9

This is:
1) an embroidery frame
2) a tapestry frame
3) a trouser press
4) a fire-screen

10

This Indian object is 25 inches in diameter. It is:
1) *a gaming table*
2) *a footstool*
3) *an urn stand*
4) *an elephant mounting block*

11

This is for holding:
1) *a marble bust* 2) *drinks*
3) *a candelabrum*
4) *flower arrangements*

12

This stand dates from:
1) *c.1650* 2) *c.1750*
3) *c.1850* 4) *c.1900*

13

Is this George III satinwood stand for use by:
1) *a musician* 2) *a lecturer*
3) *a conjurer* 4) *a seamstress*

15

Is this:
1) *a Georgian surgeon's compendium*
2) *an Edwardian dressing table*
3) *a lepidopterist's mounting table*
4) *a sewing table*

14

This is a:
1) *plant stand* 2) *washstand*
3) *winetable* 4) *cheesemaker's table*

Mirrors

Early mirrors were made of polished steel and glass mirrors were for hundreds of years a luxury item and extremely expensive. The English had a flourishing mirror manufactory at Vauxhall, and the French production of mirrors was stimulated by the demands of furnishing the Palace of Versailles, particularly the 'Hall of Mirrors'. Besides the humble 'toilet' mirror overmantel and pier 'glasses' were designed to fit in with the architectural details of grand eighteenth-century rooms.

1

The candleholders on this Queen Anne mirror are called:
1) sconces 2) tapers
3) candelabra

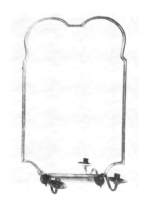

2

Three examples of mirrors to be found above:
1) sideboard 2) bath
3) fireplace 4) door
and called:
a) side b) overmantel c) pier
d) shaving

a

c

b

3

This type of mirror designed to have candles placed in front of it is called a:
1) pierglass 2) cassolette
3) wall-light 4) girandole

5

This Georgian pierglass was designed to be placed:
1) over a fireplace
2) over a bath
3) between two windows
4) in a bedroom

4

Which is the correct description:
1) a George II circular, gilt mirror
2) a Victorian carved girandola
3) a Regency eagle mirror
4) a Regency gilt convex mirror

6

What kind of mirror is this:
1) cheval 2) dressing
3) toilet 4) pier

Ceramics

Ceramics, deriving from the Greek word 'keramos', is an enormous field including the most sophisticated and beautifully designed Ming wares as well as crude terracotta utilitarian examples. As early as the Bronze Age simple and decorated pottery had achieved considerable sophistication, as excavations at Mycenae and Knossos have revealed. The Greeks brought to perfection 'black- and red-figured' pottery from the seventh to the fifth centuries BC.

China during the period of the Tang and Sung dynasties (AD618-1279) produced earthenware and stoneware pottery of increasing sophistication. It was during this period that early porcelain manufacture began, a new material consisting of white kaolin clay and felspar, which when fired at high temperatures produced a brilliant white, hard and translucent material.

Porcelain manufacture reached the heights of artistic expression under the Ming Emperors and early imports to Europe via the Middle East had an explosive impact.

In the fifteenth century a tin-glazed earthenware called 'maiolica' reached artistic maturity in Renaissance Italy, the influence of which spread to France, where it was called 'faience', and the Netherlands and England, where it came to be named 'delft-ware'. This coincided with another great wave of influence from China resulting from the import of seventeenth-century blue and white wares which were copied at Delft and other centres such as London and Bristol. In the next century Augustus the Strong of Saxony and Poland encouraged the chemist Böttger to find a European equivalent of Chinese porcelain, which took place near Dresden at a village called Meissen. Once the closely guarded secret was discovered, other manufacturers followed suit.

1

These Faenza albarellos were designed to contain:
1) oil 2) water 3) drugs 4) coffee

2

This is an example of Italian Renaissance pottery usually called:
1) Faenza 2) maiolica 3) millefiori

This type of bottle or flask is called a:
a) pilgrim b) ramshorn c) moulded d) bladder bottle

3

Tin-glazed pottery imitations of Chinese porcelain came to be known as:
1) Hague 2) Bristol 3) Delft 4) Harlem ware

4

This late C.17th ewer is:
1) Dutch 2) Irish 3) French 4) English delft

5

This plate is:
1) Dutch 2) Irish 3) English
delft
and made around:
a) 1600 b) 1690 c) 1750

7

What was this delft pot used
for:
1) holding brushes
2) growing bulbs
3) holding flowers
4) burning joss sticks

6

What is this:
1) an eyebath 2) an eggcup
3) a salt 4) a pillholder

8

This:
1) kettle tile 2) pill slab
3) vintner's label 4) butcher's slab
would have been used by:
a) an apothecary b) a cook
c) a carver d) a dyer

9

These are a type of:
1) brûle parfum 2) spoon rack
3) vase
called:
a) cassolettes b) spooners
c) flower bricks

10

What is this:
1) a sauceboat 2) a cow creamer
3) a cow boat 4) a milker

11

This Staffordshire teapot is known as:
1) marbled 2) slip
3) agate 4) onyx ware

12

This is:
1) an eggcup 2) an eyebath
3) a pillholder 4) a vase

13

This Longton Hall:
1) punch bowl 2) two-handled cup
3) loving cup 4) wassail cup
is decorated to imitate which style:
a) famille rose b) famille noire
c) famille jaune d) famille verte

14

This is a:
1) spoon tray 2) wickholder
3) sauceboat 4) taperholder

15

These four Plymouth figures represent:
1) the four seasons
2) the four winds
3) the four continents

16

Match caption to illustration:
1) Derby ice pail
2) pastille burner
3) Longton Hall sauceboat
4) Worcester cress dish and stand
5) Chamberlain's Worcester honey pot
6) spill-vase
7) Worcester sifter spoon
8) Derby tureen

a

b

c

d

e

f

g

h

17

The type of decoration on this Staffordshire miniature cradle is called:
1) *slop* 2) *slip* 3) *crosshatch*
4) *tammed*

18

This type of jug is called a:
1) *Darby* 2) *Billy* 3) *Wendy*
4) *Toby* jug

19

This Worcester 'fable' dish was painted by:
1) *J.H. O'Neale* 2) *James Giles*
3) *Henry O'Cready*
4) *J. Höroldt*
How much is it worth:
a) *£200-300* b) *£800-1000*
c) *£2000-3000*

20

This Bow mug is decorated with what is known as the:
1) *long Liza* 2) *pinecone*
3) *golfer-and-caddy*
4) *fantastic bird*
   pattern

21

This Chelsea plate painted with botanical studies is named after which famous C.18th naturalist:
1) *Carl Linnaeus* 2) *John Martyn*
3) *Sir Hans Sloane*
4) *Sir Joseph Banks*

22

This Liverpool tankard is decorated with:
1) *painted* 2) *transfer printed*
3) *etched* 4) *stencilled* motifs

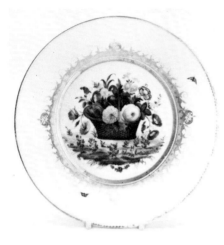

23

This Swansea plate is named after which C.19th philanthropist:
1) *Baroness Burdett-Coutts*
2) *Florence Nightingale*
3) *George Peabody*
4) *General Booth*

24

The pattern on this Worcester dish is known as the :
1) *Earl of Coventry*
2) *jolly squire* 3) *blind earl*
4) *rose-leaf*

25

Who decorated this Worcester teapot:
1) *J. H. O'Neale* 2) *James Giles*
3) *William Billingsley*
4) *Harry Davies*

26

This type of elaborate foliate and floral decoration is called:
1) *bosley* 2) *arbour*
3) *bocage* 4) *trellis*

27

This tureen is in a type of stoneware called:
1) *Chaffers' clinker* 2) *Parian ware*
3) *Mason's ironstone* 4) *Etruria*

29

These figures are known as:
1) *Derby dwarfs*
2) *Mansion House dwarfs*
3) *Punches*
4) *Callot Comicals*

28

What is this type of teaset called:
1) *a unitaire* 2) *a 'misogynist'*
3) *a solitaire*

30

What is this:
1) a nécessaire 2) a reticule
3) an inkstand 4) a housewife

31

This type of biscuit porcelain
was first made by:
1) Meissen 2) Derby
3) William Ball
4) Josiah Wedgwood

32

These objects were all made at
which famous French
porcelain manufacturers:
1) Rouen 2) Vincennes
3) Mennecy 4) Sèvres

34

The form of this Marseilles:
1) soft paste 2) hard paste
3) ironstone 4) faience
bowl is taken from an original
in which material:
a) silver b) gold c) enamel
d) pewter

33

This is a Sèvres:
1) coffee cup and saucer
2) tea cup and saucer
3) coffee can and saucer
4) chocolate cup and saucer

35

This type of Japanese-inspired decoration is called:
1) *uke-jo-e* 2) *arita* 3) *kanagawa*
4) *kakiemon*

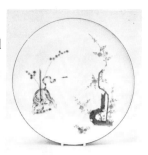

36

This is a Meissen:
1) *butter cooler* 2) *bonbonnière*
3) *sugarbox* 4) *muffinbox*

37

This is a Meissen:
1) *schnapps flask* 2) *spirit decanter*
3) *oil cruet* 4) *tea caddy*

38

What was this St Cloud container for:
1) *pot-pourri* 2) *smelling salts*
3) *incense* 4) *pomander*

39

This Kloster Veilsdorf figure, 'Le Turc amoureux', is a character in which famous drama:
1) *La Comédie Humaine*
2) *Le Jeu de l'Amour et du Hasard*
3) *La Commedia dell'Arte*

40

This type of cup and saucer designed to avoid spilling the contents is called a:
1) *vieilleuse* 2) *trembleuse*
3) *tricoteuse* 4) 'socket' tea-cup

41

Match the description to the
illustration:
1) nécessaire 2) bodkin case
3) chestnut basket 4) cane handle
5) thimble 6) scent bottle and
  stopper 7) pipe bowl
8) cheese dish 9) foot bath

c

b

d

e

f

g

h

i

42

What are these fat children
with wings called:
*1) cherubs 2) cupids 3) amorini
4) putti*

43

After which excavated city is
this type of porcelain named:
*1) Herculaneum 2) Pasargadae
3) Troy 4) Pompeii*

44

What was contained in these
little pots:
*1) jelly 2) soup 3) custard
4) brandy*

45

This type of slightly metallic
shiny decoration is called:
*1) pearlware 2) lacquer 3) lustre
4) brightware*

46

This is a Minton majolica:
*1) table fountain 2) oyster stand
3) centrepiece 4) mussel bank*

47

This Liverpool delft jug with
pierced neck and three spouts
is known as:
*1) a puzzle-jug 2) an enigma-jug
3) a sportive-jug 4) an
abstinence-pot*

48

What is this:
*1) a Wedgwood night light
2) a Wedgwood wall light
3) a Wedgwood chandelier
4) a Wedgwood hall lantern*

50

This exhibition piece by Minton's is decorated by M. L. Solon in a technique called:
1) *pâte-sur-pâte*
2) *couche-après-couche*
3) *verre églomisé* 4) *bisque*

49

What is this chimney-piece made out of:
1) *salt-glazed stoneware*
2) *Mason's ironstone* 3) *coalstone*
4) *Arita porcelain*

51

This Royal Worcester jar was made by:
1) *John Atkins* 2) *George Owen*
3) *John Martin* 4) *William De Morgan*

53

This is an example of:
1) *Sunderland lustre* 2) *Loetz ware*
3) *De Morgan lustre*
4) *fairyland lustre*

52

This basket is a good example of which Irish late C.19th porcelain factory:
1) *Belleek* 2) *Delamain*
3) *Waterford* 4) *Penrose*

54

These humorous birds are typical of the work of which brothers:
1) *Passenger* 2) *Maxwell*
3) *Martin* 4) *Bugatti*

55

When was this Royal Doulton jug made:
1) *1920* 2) *1945* 3) *1960* 4) *1984*

56

Is this 'pagoda figure' Chinese or European?

57

This figure of the goddess Guan Yin in porcelain is known as:
1) *blanc-de-Chine*
2) *Chinese undecorated*
3) *blanc-et-blanc* 4) *creamware*

58

This plate with a European coat of arms is an example of:
1) *Chinoiserie* 2) *Chinese import*
3) *Chinese export* 4) *famille verte*

59

This type of Chinese plate in various shades of sea-green is called:
1) *calcedony* 2) *celadon*
3) *calcifuge* 4) *caledon*

60

This brightly coloured famille verte vase was made in:
1) *Birmingham*
2) *honour of an emperor*
3) *the Yung Cheng period*
4) *the Kang Xi period*

61

The decoration on this plate is typical of the work of:
1) *Clarice Cliff* 2) *Jean Luce*
3) *Charlotte Rhead*
4) *William De Morgan*

62

These blue and white objects standing 19 inches high date from the late Qing dynasty and are valued at £2000-3000. Are they:
1) wine casks 2) ceremonial drums
3) pearl fishers' floats 4) garden seats

63

This Copeland bust is made of hard, white unglazed material known as:
1) Copeland stone
2) Athenian ware
3) Paris marble 4) Parian ware

64

These vases, dated *c.*1880, bear a printed mark of crown over initials. They are:
1) Crown Derby
2) Royal Doulton
3) Meissen imperial
4) Chelsea Queen

65

This:
1) Ralph Wood 2) Enoch Wood
3) John Turner
figure dates from:
a) c.1725 b) c.1780
c) c.1812 d) c.1840

66

This green, gold and purple lustre parrot is by:
1) Meissen 2) Worcester
3) Zsolnay 4) Wedgwood

Clocks & Watches

Although civilisations before our own developed clocks with mechanical parts – notably those of Ancient Egypt and China – the first fully mechanical clock is believed to have been the one erected in a Milan church in 1335. Another, installed in Salisbury Cathedral some fifty years later, has been restored and can still be seen working.

The earliest 'general-purpose' clocks used in England were lantern clocks, made in considerable numbers during the sixteenth and seventeenth centuries. These were supplanted by longcase clocks, the earliest of which are really no more than lantern clocks set in a long case, and bracket clocks.

The earliest bracket clocks were set in cases which strongly resembled the upper part of longcase clocks and often incorporated a repeat mechanism.

As a means of raising revenue for the Napoleonic War, William Pitt imposed a tax on clocks and watches in 1797. Almost overnight the English clock-making industry went into decline and, although the tax was lifted within the year, thousands of clockmakers were put out of work. It is a consequence of this that the 'tavern' clock became known as the 'Act of Parliament' clock, it being the belief of some that people got rid of their own clocks and watches in order to avoid the tax, and relied on large clocks put on public display for their personal timekeeping. In truth this is hardly likely, since such public clocks had been in service for some fifty years already.

1
What is this instrument:
1) a timepiece 2) a chronometer
3) a regulator

2
What would you do when altering the hands on this clock:
1) slide the hood up
2) open the door
3) turn the key in the back

3
What type of clock is this:
1) cartel 2) carriage
3) alarm 4) bracket

4
Is the top called a:
1) dome 2) lid 3) basket
4) double-basket

5
What is the correct term for this type of clock:
1) grandfather 2) grandmother
3) longcase

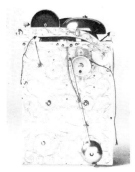

7

What type of bracket clock is this:
1) balloon 2) ball 3) bullseye
4) pedestal

6

This is the engraved backplate of a clock by Daniel Quare. It has a fine walnut case and is worth between:
1) £2000-3000 2) £5000-10000
3) £10000-15000 4) £20000-25000

a

b

c

d

10

Place these clocks in chronological order according to style:

g

e

f

8

Is this clock:
1) Swiss 2) French
3) English 4) German

9

Is the mechanism which works the clock called a:
1) verge escapement 2) regulator
3) movement 4) anchor escapement

11

Match the illustration to the description:
1) *garniture*
2) *lighthouse clock*
3) *lyre clock*
4) *mantel chronometer*

a

b

c

d

12

a

b

a) Chronometer carriage clock, M. F. Dent, London. Value £3000-4000.
b) Brass grande sonnerie carriage clock, Louis Fernier & Frère, Paris. Value £700-800. Why is **a** so much more valuable:
1) *French carriage clocks were mass-produced*
2) *English carriage clocks were mass-produced*
3) *English carriage clocks are rarer*

13

This German tabernacle clock is dated:
1) *c.1500* 2) *c.1600* 3) *c.1700*
4) *c.1800*

14

This London-made watch of *c.*1770 is mounted on a:
1) *watch belt* 2) *bracket*
3) *key-ring* 4) *châtelaine*

15

How much is it worth:
1) *£300-500* 2) *£2000-3000*
3) *£3000-4000* 4) *£10000-12000*

16

Fit the illustration to the description:
1) cuckoo clock 2) sedan clock
3) lantern clock
4) Act of Parliament clock
5) stopwatch

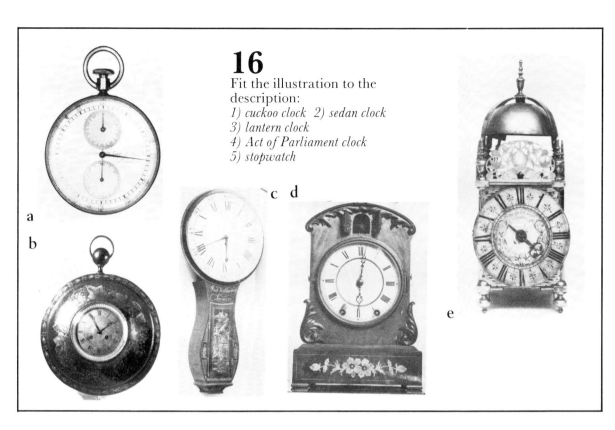

a

b

c   d

e

18

What period:
1) George II 2) Louis XV
3) Régence 4) Regency

17

The movement of this clock is concealed in the base. It is known as:
1) a mystery clock
2) a conundrum clock
3) a pillar clock
4) a machine-perdue clock

19

This clock is of the type known as:
1) a drop-dial wall-clock
2) a Black Forest clock
3) a Vienna Regulator
4) a Birmingham eight-day clock

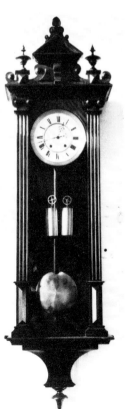

20

This brass skeleton clock is of the type known as:
1) *Lichfield Cathedral*
2) *Winchester Cathedral*
3) *Norwich Cathedral*
4) *York Minster*

21

This:
1) *bracket* 2) *hanging wall*
3) *cabinet*
clock dates from:
a) *c.1400* b) *c.1500* c) *c.1600*
d) *c.1700*

22

Fit the description to the illustrations:
1) *a German early C.17th verge watch*
2) *a silver pair-cased verge watch, early C.18th*
3) *a pair-cased verge watch with nautical dial 1779*
4) *mid C.19th open-faced pocket watch*
5) *a hunting cased stopwatch*

a

b

c

d

e

23

This watch was made for which market:
1) Bohemian 2) Irish
3) American 4) Turkish

24

When was this desk clock made:
1) 1800 2) 1890 3) 1935 4) 1955

25

How much is this 18c. gold automatic perpetual calendar moonphase watch by Patek Philippe worth:
1) £700-800 2) £7000-8000
3) £12000-15000

26

What is this:
1) a cuckoo clock 2) a watch holder
3) a house clock
4) a tabernacle clock

27

Where would this chronometer have been used:
1) on a train 2) in a stock exchange
3) on board ship 4) in a submarine

28

What is the 'hand' of a sundial called:
1) finger 2) gnomon 3) sun stick
4) traverse

Scientific Instruments

In the course of time many thousands of scientific instruments have been preserved by interested persons. Fortunately for modern collectors, the eighteenth and nineteenth centuries saw a tremendous popular interest in science and discovery, with a corresponding proliferation of instruments designed to assist the study of everything from the motions of the universe at large to the microscopic components of matter.

Although some members of a number of professional bodies are nowadays keen collectors of instruments used by their predecessors – most notably doctors and dentists – there is ample scope for those attracted by the quaint and curious. And even the macabre.

The barometer was originally developed during the explosive increase in scientific discovery and experiment that took place during the seventeenth century as a means of observing the relationship between air pressure and altitude. It was only by chance that it was noticed how a change in the weight, or pressure, of the air was connected with a corresponding change in the weather.

Although domestic barometers are engraved with the familiar weather indicators – rain, change, fair and so on, these are relatively meaningless. It is the increase or decrease in pressure at any given time that may be used to forecast the weather, and a drop from 'very dry' to 'fair' is as sure an indicator of rain as a drop from 'fair' to 'rain'. In fact, the only reason for such indicators to be on the dial is that fashion demands them!

Early barometers all contain a tube (or 'column') of mercury, usually a little under 36 inches long, sealed at the top and standing in a cistern of mercury. A later development dispensed with the cistern, and the tube was bent like an umbrella handle, open at the short end. By the end of the seventeenth century, barometers were widely available, and the quality of the instrument was usually reflected in the quality of the case.

The banjo or wheel barometer originated in France and was adopted in Britain during the late eighteenth century, the style of the case reflecting contemporary architectural features in its details.

1
What is this late C.16th compendium dial by Erasmus Habermel worth:
1) £1500-2500 2) £2000-3000
3) £8000-12000 4) £15000-20000

2
Is this a Chinese:
1) *sundial/compass*
2) *divination board*
3) *astrological computer*
4) *adding machine*

3
What type of microscope:
1) *tripod* 2) *Culpeper*
3) *Johnson & Johnson* 4) *Erasinus*

5

What is this instrument:
1) a microscope 2) a sextant
3) a theodolite 4) a compass
Is it used to:
a) magnify samples
b) survey changes in ground level
c) measure the equator
d) measure the arc of Venus

4

What is this instrument:
1) a microscope 2) a reflector
3) a solar microscope
4) a heliotrope

6

What is this:
1) a pocket globe
2) a pocket calculator
3) an astrologer's ball
4) a celestial globe

8

What was this instrument used for:
1) measuring mine shafts
2) geological samples
3) a ship's log
4) building roads

7

Who would have used this C.18th dial:
1) a surveyor 2) a miner
3) a ship's captain 4) an astronomer

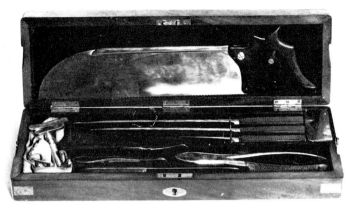

9

Was this set of instruments
used for:
1) *making furniture*
2) *amputating limbs*
3) *butchering meat*
4) *plumbing*

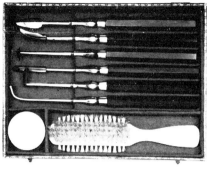

10

Would these instruments have
been used by:
1) *a dentist* 2) *a vet*
3) *a doctor* 4) *an intaglio carver*

11

Were these used to:
1) *sterilise instruments*
2) *stretch gloves* 3) *deliver babies*
4) *pick up flat irons*

12

The carving on this barometer
is typical of which period:
1) *mid C.18th* 2) *early C.19th*
3) *William IV* 4) *late Victorian*

13

What type of barometer is this:
1) *marine* 2) *ball-tube*
3) *stick* 4) *siphon*

15

This is a:
1) *log finder* 2) *way-wiser*
3) *milometer*
and was used to measure:
a) *distance covered overland*
b) *speed of horse-drawn carriage*
c) *power generated by a watermill*

14

What musical instrument is
associated with this type of
barometer:
1) *banjo* 2) *lute* 3) *guitar*
4) *violin*

16

This is a C.16th German:
1) coding device 2) sextant
3) quadrant 4) astrolabe

17

These protractors are for measuring:
1) distance
2) diameters of solid spheres
3) angles 4) weight

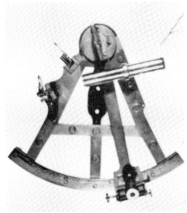

18

Who would use this:
1) a bombardier 2) a piano tuner
3) a navigator 4) a surveyor

19

This is:
1) a perpetual calendar
2) an astrological chart
3) a teaching aid
4) a music transposer

20

Is this a:
1) reflecting 2) refracting
3) nautical 4) prismatic
telescope

21

What is this:
1) an acetylene lamp
2) a spray inhaler 3) a sinus cleanser
4) a blood transfuser

Photographic

Although the first permanent photographic image was achieved in 1826, it was some time before photography as such became a viable proposition. The first cameras of collecting interest are the 'wet-plate' models of 1840 to 1880. During most of the nineteenth century, scientific interest was held more by the chemical aspects of photography than by the technical development of the camera itself as a functioning piece of apparatus. For this reason, cameras changed relatively little throughout the period, despite the introduction of 'dry' plates. It was only when, in the first half of the present century (aided considerably by the demands made on photography during the two World Wars), relatively high-speed films were developed, that cameras began to show great technical improvement.

Millions of folding cameras were marketed by Kodak as soon as the roll film brought photography within reach of the masses. These cameras, although interesting, are so plentiful that they change hands very cheaply nowadays. More sought after are stereo cameras and early models of Leicas, Rolleis, Contax and Zeiss, and the curiously disguised 'detective' cameras which were in vogue during the 1920s.

In recent years there has been a marked increase in the interest taken in photographs. Of those taken prior to 1870, almost all are of interest from a purely technical point of view. After that date, when dry plates were introduced, photography found many more devotees; hence many more photographs were taken. These retain interest today according to their artistic merit or subject matter but, since most photographs from this period seem to have been poorly composed and of subjects whose interest did not extend outside the family circle, relatively few have any significant cash value.

1
This Fores Phenakistoscope was published in 1833. It is an early form of:
1) card game 2) design for plates
3) magic lantern 4) cine camera

2
Is this called:
1) a table stereoscope
2) a diorama
3) a patent spectroscope
4) a magic lantern

3
When was this camera produced:
1) c.1830 2) c.1880
3) c.1910 4) c.1920

4
Was this camera called:
1) a telescop rear lense
2) a telephot button
3) a decrease lense
4) a telephote

5
Is this a:
1) wet plate 2) dry plate
3) ¼ plate 4) full plate
5) ½ plate wet plate
camera

Silver

Silverwares tend to have a rather precarious existence; a condition brought about by fluctuations in the commodity value of silver and vagaries of taste and fashion.

Any given article made wholly or partly of silver has, in effect, a double value; firstly that of the amount of precious metal used in its making – the scrap or 'melt' value – and secondly, the value set upon it as a piece of craftsmanship. In times of domestic crisis, or as a consequence of a steep rise in the world price of silver, the value of the metal may often be felt to far outweigh the 'heritage' value.

1

Match the following descriptions to the illustrations:
1) *cake basket* 2) *tea caddy*
3) *épergne* 4) *castors*
5) *invalid feeder* 6) *chalice*
7) *argyle* 8) *centrepiece*
9) *soap box* 10) *wine coaster*
11) *soup tureen*

a

b

c

d

e

h

f

g

k

i

j

2

This castor was made by the most renowned silversmith of Huguenot origin working in England. Was his name:
1) *Philip Rollos*
2) *David Tanqueray*
3) *Paul de Lamerie*
4) *Paul Crespin*

3

This set of George III candlesticks are loaded; does that mean:
1) *they are made of pure silver*
2) *they are especially thick at the base*
3) *the base has been filled with lead*
4) *the hollow body has been topped with ballast*

Does this make them more desirable from a collector's point of view:
a) yes b) no

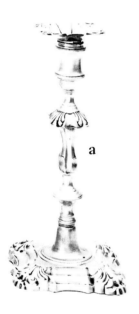

4

Place these candlesticks in chronological order:

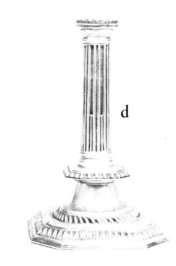

5

Is the type of engraved decoration on this tea caddy known as:
1) *bright cut* 2) *dot cut*
3) *punch cut* 4) *twinkle cut*

6

This type of stand to support a dish is associated with which country:
1) *England* 2) *Germany*
3) *Ireland* 4) *Russia*
5) *Sweden*

8

Put a date to this style:
1) *1782* 2) *1840* 3) *1890* 4) *1913*

7

Would you have used this silver case with hinged lid dated 1844 for your:
1) *spectacles* 2) *money* 3) *matches*
4) *calling cards* 5) *receipts*

9

Are these scissors for:
1) *grapes* 2) *paper* 3) *needlework*
4) *asparagus*

11

Was this used for hot:
*1) rum 2) posset
3) cordial 4) brandy*

12

Would this service have been used:
*1) when travelling 2) on campaign
3) 1 and 2 4) in hospital*

10

What was this object used for:
*1) lighting fires 2) snuffing candles
3) trimming wicks 4) 2 and 3*

13

Place these services in
chronological order:

a

b

c

d

14

Was this for:
1) mulled wine 2) chocolate
3) coffee 4) soup

15

This was made by the famous
Russian jeweller:
1) Morozov 2) Khlebnikov
3) Fabergé 4) Sazikov
to hold:
a) sweetbread b) caviar
c) bortsch d) jam

16

This centrepiece is modelled
after:
1) Nelson's Column
2) the London Monument
3) the lighthouse at Rhodes
4) Trajan's Column

17

This pedestal
trencher/columnar salt was
made in:
1) c.1550 2) c.1650 3) c.1750
and is worth around:
a) £500 b) £2500 c) £5500
d) £10000

18

What is this type of teapot
usually called:
1) ball 2) bullet 3) melon
It is associated with which
period:
a) late C.17th b) early C.18th
c) late C.19th

19

Match the town to the mark:
1) York 2) Birmingham
3) Sheffield 4) Edinburgh
5) Dublin

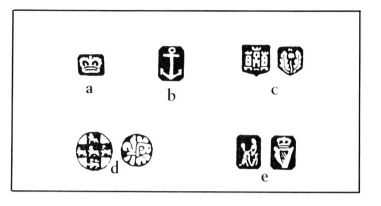

20

Match the handle to its pattern:
1) King's 2) Queen's
3) Fiddle Thread 4) Hourglass
5) Fiddle Thread and Shell

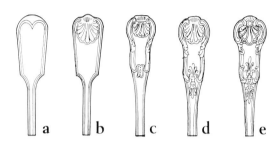

21

Silver and ivory figures of this type are typically:
1) Swedish 2) German
3) Portuguese 4) Swiss

22

These serving spoons are:
1) Austrian 2) English 3) Dutch
4) Russian

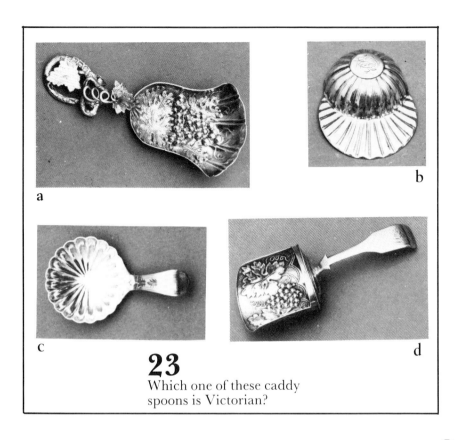

a

b

c

d

23

Which one of these caddy spoons is Victorian?

24

This Dutch silver object is 15 inches long. It is:
1) *a fish server*
2) *a peacock feather fan handle*
3) *a punch strainer*
4) *a hot chestnut server*

25

This is known as:
1) *a porridge spoon*
2) *a seal-top spoon*
3) *a trefid spoon*
4) *a rat-tail spoon*

26

This snuffbox is marked for Birmingham, 1828, was it made by:
1) *Omar Ramsden*
2) *Nathaniel Mills*
3) *Paul de Lamerie*
4) *Paul Storr*

Glass/Paperweights

Although a certain amount of glass was made continuously from the time of the Roman occupation, the British glass industry produced virtually no work of note until, in 1676, George Ravenscroft discovered how to combine lead with silica and potash to create lead glass. Prior to that time, Venice had held pride of place among the world's glassmakers, producing fine, light glasswares of greenish soda metal ('metal' is the term used to describe the actual glass as a substance, as opposed to the articles into which it is made).

The new lead metal was softer, heavier and more lustrous than soda metal, lending itself admirably to the production of table wares and drinking glasses. Being less brittle, it allowed for thicker, more durable articles to be made. Glasswares at that time were sold according to their weight – 12d per pound (5p per .55 kilo) – regardless of other factors such as style or quality of workmanship.

2

This black bottle *c.*1720 is of the type called:
1) demijohn 2) onion
3) gourd 4) port

1

Bottles of this type are known as:
1) longneck 2) clinker
3) globe-and-shaft 4) onion
What date is it:
a) c.1400 b) c.1550 c) c.1650
d) c.1720

4

This German humpen is decorated in:
1) cold painting 2) pâte-sur-pâte
3) enamel 4) sulphide

3

This type of German glass is called a:
1) roemer 2) kuggel
3) Rhine glass 4) stangen
The little blobs of glass round the stem are known as:
a) raspberries b) strawberries
c) nodules d) prunts

5

This Dutch C.17th glass is decorated with:
1) a needle
2) an abrasive wheel
3) a diamond 4) a drill

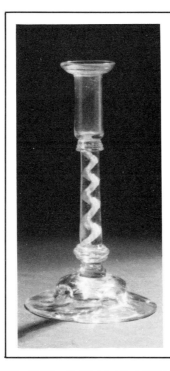

6

This is a:
1) candlestick 2) taperstick
3) wickholder 4) cherootholder

7

The stem has a corkscrew of:
1) air threads 2) metal threads
3) enamel threads 4) mercury threads

8

What sort of glass is this:
1) toastmaster's 2) firing
3) toddy 4) tot

9

With which movement is the engraving on the glass connected:
1) Hanoverian 2) Jacobean
3) Jacobite

10

This French scent bottle is made in opaque glass called:
1) opal 2) carnival
3) vaseline 4) opaline

11

What was drunk in a glass like this:
1) cordial 2) firewater
3) brandy 4) 2 and 3

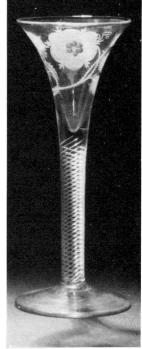

14

This is a Webb's cameo:
1) *scent flask* 2) *hip flask*
3) *pocket telescope*
4) *pipe-cleaner holder*

12

This vase was carved in a
technique called:
1) *intaglio* 2) *cameo*
3) *bas-relief* 4) *intarsien*

13

What it is worth:
1) *£500-700* 2) *£2000-3000*
3) *£8000-12000*

15

This bowl was traditionally
made in:
1) *Wales* 2) *Scotland*
3) *Cornwall* 4) *Ireland*

16

The shape is called:
1) *boat* 2) *canoe*
3) *basket* 4) *ovoid*

17

And it is worth between:
1) *£50-100* 2) *£300-400*
3) *£3000-4000*

19

This Bohemian goblet *c.*1860 is
made by a technique called:
1) *flashing* 2) *overlay*
3) *sandwich* 4) *cire-perdue*

18

What is this called:
1) *a wineglass rinser*
2) *a wineglass cooler*
3) *a finger bowl*
4) *1 and 2*

20

This Baccarat paperweight is made up of many tiny canes known as:
1) mirafiori 2) vermicelli
3) millefiori 4) coralwork
It also has a date cane. The most common one is:
a) 1845 b) 1846 c) 1848 d) 1850

21

This is a Clichy:
1) swirl 2) radial
3) catherine wheel
weight
How much is it worth:
a) £50-100 b) £350-450
c) £500-700

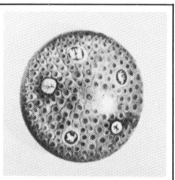

22

The ground of this type of weight is called:
1) polyp 2) coral 3) carpet

23

How much is it worth:
1) £500-700 2) £1500-2000
3) £2500-3500

24

This is a St Louis:
1) basket 2) mushroom
3) crown
weight

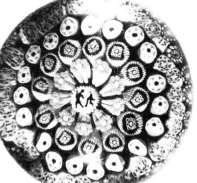

25

This St Louis concentric weight is worth between:
1) £20-30 2) £200-300
3) £600-800 4) £1000-1500

26

This overlay glass decanter is:
1) *Bristol* 2) *Belgian*
3) *Belfast* 4) *Bohemian*

28

This is a Sunderland:
1) *flagon* 2) *toaster* 3) *bucket*
4) *rummer*

27

This façon de Venise glass
cruet was made in:
1) *Cataluña* 2) *Venice* 3) *Orrefors*
4) *Nancy*

29

This wineglass is probably
from the South Netherlands.
Its date is:
1) *mid C.15th* 2) *early C.16th*
3) *late C.17th* 4) *early C.18th*

30

The stem of this goblet is of
which form:
1) *baluster* 2) *inverted baluster*
3) *pearknop* 4) *inverted pearknop*

Art Nouveau/Arts & Crafts

The Art Nouveau movement was far more than just a change of stylistic direction. Its philosophical roots were derived from Japan and embraced all aspects of art and design from the Dance to the manufacture of the humblest of domestic goods. Since it involved a change of attitude and an attempt to interpret nature, there was no single Art Nouveau style, and a number of national and regional characteristics emerged.

Broadly speaking, the more northern exponents favoured rather angular, austere shapes, while those from southern areas, notably France, developed a far more exotic and sinuous approach. Following the Paris Exhibition of 1860, public appreciation of the new art forms was instantaneous, and manufacturers were quick to respond to demand. At best, the Art Nouveau movement produced some superb designs beautifully executed; at worst, articles of inferior manufacture were applied with motifs of stylised decoration quite inappropriate to the form.

2
When was this buffet made:
1) c.1860 2) c.1880 3) c.1920

3
How much is it worth:
1) £200-300 2) £500-700
3) £2000-3000 4) £5000-7000

1
This chair and the fabric on it was designed by:
1) *William De Morgan*
2) *Liberty & Co.*
3) *L. C. Tiffany* 4) *George Jack*

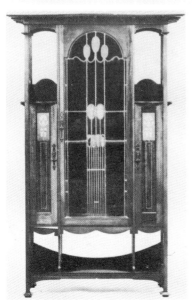

5
This:
1) *book rest* 2) *cake stand*
3) *étagère*
was designed by:
a) *Louis Majorelle*
b) *Bernhard Pankok*
c) *Carlo Bugatti*

4
This is an Art Nouveau:
1) *display cabinet* 2) *vitrine*
3) *bookcase* 4) *music cabinet*

6

How much are this desk and chair worth:
1) £100-150 2) £500-700
3) £1000-1500

7

This stained glass window and oak side chair were designed by the same person. Was he:
1) Emile Gallé
2) Charles Rennie Mackintosh
3) Frank Lloyd Wright
4) William Morris

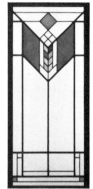

8

His nationality:
1) English 2) Scots
3) Welsh 4) American

10

This table lamp by:
1) Gallé 2) Marinot 3) Daum
is worth between:
a) £250-350 b) £1000-1500
c) £5000-7000 d) £10000+

9

This vase was designed by:
1) Emile Gallé 2) Daum
3) Muller Frères
The technique is:
a) carved overlay b) cire-perdue
c) carved cameo
It is worth:
i) £20-30 ii) £250-350
iii) £800-1200 iv) £1500-2000

11

This vase is from the Austrian factory:
1) Kothgasser 2) Lobmeyr
3) Loetz 4) Steiner
which is famous for the use of:
a) plastic form b) iridescence
c) colour contrast

12

This iridescent vase is by a famous American designer. Was he:
1) *Carder* 2) *Libbey* 3) *Tiffany*
4) *Cartier*

13

These are bronze:
1) *wall lights* 2) *torchères*
3) *coat racks* 4) *candelabra*

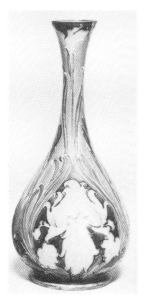

14

This Moorcroft vase was made:
1) *c.1880* 2) *c.1890* 3) *c.1900*
4) *c.1908*

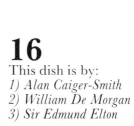

15

This Royal Doulton vase was named by the factory in homage to which Chinese dynasty:
1) *Tang* 2) *Ming* 3) *Sung*

16

This dish is by:
1) *Alan Caiger-Smith*
2) *William De Morgan*
3) *Sir Edmund Elton*

17

Who made this stoneware vase:
1) *Doulton, Lambeth*
2) *Royal Doulton*
3) *Doulton, Burslem*

18

How much would a pair of these Doulton vases be worth:
1) *£200-300* 2) *£500-700*
3) *£800-1200* 4) *£3000-4000*

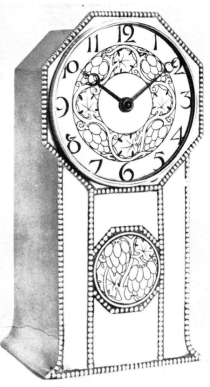

19

This clock was made by:
1) *Breguet* 2) *Liberty & Co.*
3) *Tiffany* 4) *C. R. Mackintosh*

20

Of what is the surround to this clock made:
1) *Pratt ware* 2) *stoneware*
3) *majolica* 4) *Parian ware*

21

This lithograph is by:
1) *Constantin Meunier*
2) *Arthur Rackham*
3) *Mabel Lucie Attwell*
4) *Alphonse Mucha*

22

Who designed this polished pewter photograph frame:
1) *Hugo Leven*
2) *Archibald Knox*
3) *Harry Silver*
4) *Oliver Baker*

23

This is a silver and glass:
1) claret jug 2) coffee jug
3) punch pot 4) cold-tea pot

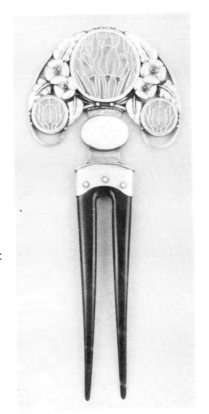

24

Is this an Arts and Crafts:
1) menu holder 2) toothpick
3) tie-pin 4) hairpin

25

This bronze plaque is signed:
1) N. Fournier 2) C. Bugatti
3) A. Rodin 4) C. R. Mackintosh

26

The angels on this Foley
'intarsio' vase are of which
school:
1) Renaissance 2) Realist
3) Pre-Raphaelite 4) Impressionist

27

This silver-plated pitcher and
bowl are marked 'WMF'.
Where were they made:
1) France 2) Austria
3) Scotland 4) Wales

Art Deco

Following the rapid commercialism of the more appealing elements of Art Nouveau styles, designers began to concentrate on the decorative effects of curve and line expressed in geometric form. They were aided by the development of new materials and methods of manufacture.

In order to focus attention on form, much use was made of glass and other high-finish material which often served to emphasise rather than disguise the function of the article.

The term 'Art Deco' derives from the Exposition des Arts Décoratifs in Paris in 1925 and, as with Art Nouveau, there is no single style or form. Indeed, individual designers associated with the movement often produced articles of such widely differing styles that it is not uncommon these days to determine that an object is or is not 'Art Deco' simply because it was or was not made by a particular designer or factory.

1

When was this tea set made:
1) 1900 2) 1919 3) 1938
4) 1954

2

This tea service was designed by:
1) Clarice Cliff 2) Lucie Rie
3) Bernard Leach 4) Hans Coper

3

What is this:
1) a whatnot 2) an étagère
3) a tea trolley 4) a jardinière

4

This pâte de verre cordial set is by:
1) Daum 2) Argy-Rousseau
3) Tiffany 4) Sowerby

6

In what way are these two
dressing tables typical of the
Art Deco style:
1) they both have spiky legs
2) their geometric form
3) use of mirror plate
4) 2 and 3

5

When was this chair made:
1) c.1900 2) c.1935 3) c.1940
4) c.1960

8

Is this a silver:
1) card case 2) cigarette case
3) spectacle case

7

What is this:
1) a side table 2) a coffee table
3) a display cabinet
When was it made:
a) 1900s b) 1920s c) 1930s
d) 1950s

9

What is this:
1) a hip flask
2) an early vacuum flask
3) a cocktail shaker
4) a champagne cooler

10

This figurine is made out of:
1) *porcelain* 2) *silver*
3) *ivory and silver*
4) *ivory and bronze*
What date is it:
a) *c.1890* b) *c.1910*
c) *c.1930* d) *c.1950*

11

This figurine was made by:
1) *D. H. Chiparus*
2) *Ferdinand Preiss*
3) *Professor Poertzel*

12

How much is it worth:
1) *£150-200* 2) *£800-1000*
3) *£1200-1400*

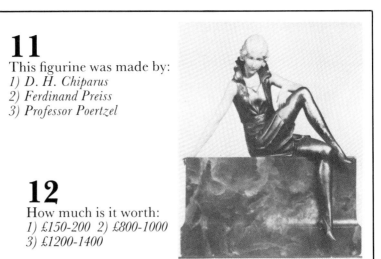

13

This vase by:
1) *Royal Doulton* 2) *Clarice Cliff*
3) *Wedgwood* 4) *Liberty & Co.*
is painted with the:
a) *daffodil* b) *anemone*
c) *crocus* d) *forget-me-not*
pattern

14

The frame to this clock is in
what material:
1) *brass* 2) *pewter* 3) *enamel*
4) *glass*

15

This figure is by:
1) *R. Lalique* 2) *Orrefors*
3) *Steuben* 4) *Lobmeyr*
What is it worth:
a) *£100-200* b) *£1000-1500*
c) *£3000-4000*

16
This vase was made by
Orrefors in:
1) Denmark 2) Germany
3) Sweden 4) Norway

17
This is a Lalique:
1) pendant 2) goldfish bowl
3) hanging shade
4) hanging jardinière

18
What is this:
1) a brooch 2) a tie-pin
3) a menu holder 4) a knife rest

19
This glass figure was made by
René Lalique. He was not a
notable designer of:
1) jewellery 2) car mascots
3) scent flasks 4) art furniture

20
This is a Lalique:
1) table lamp 2) inkwell
3) doorknob 4) car mascot

21

This pottery head was made by:

1) Clarice Cliff 2) Rodin
3) Susie Cooper 4) Picasso

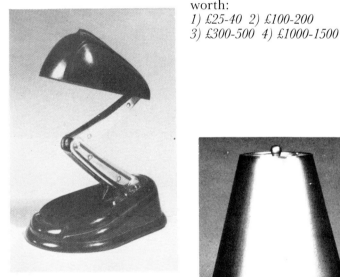

22

This 14-inch diameter glass charger is by Lalique. It is worth:

1) £25-40 2) £100-200
3) £300-500 4) £1000-1500

23

This bakelite and metal lamp was made:

1) c.1915 2) c.1930
3) c.1945 4) c.1950

24

About when was this cutlery made by Georg Jensen:

1) 1900s 2) 1920s
3) 1930s 4) 1940s

25

Is this glass and chrome table lamp:

1) Swedish 2) Persian 3) French
4) Greek

Metalware

The term metalware is generally used to include all base (i.e. non-precious) metals, including iron and steel, copper, brass and bronze, pewter and spelter. These are the metals used for the manufacture of functional objects, and sometimes things of extraordinary beauty.

Unlike precious metal, which is usually marked with precise dating guides, the majority of base metal objects present a more difficult challenge to the collector. Methods of construction, amount of wear, patination, finish; it is these that provide the clues to those who are prepared to devote the time – and the money – to gaining the necessary experience.

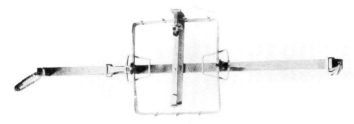

2

This trap was used for catching:
1) poachers 2) foxes
3) rabbits 4) bears

1

These German brass boxes were made to contain:
1) snuff 2) pills
3) tobacco 4) pens

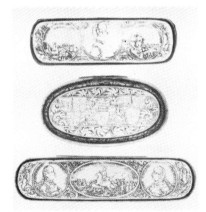

3

This C.17th brass dish was used in a:
1) convent 2) family home
3) lawcourt 4) church

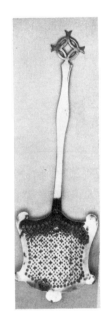

4

What is this:
1) a toasting fork 2) a sieve
3) a skimmer 4) a strainer

5

This Victorian 28-inch long cast metal lion was designed as a:
1) door stop 2) chenet
3) fire dog 4) statuette

6

This early C.18th cooking pot
is called:
1) a trivet 2) a skillet
3) a cresset 4) a tripod

7

This lead badge was placed on
the outside of a house in the
C.18th by:
1) the local council
2) the local preservation society
3) the fire insurance company
4) the anti-slave trade movement

8

In which part of a house was
this lantern designed to hang:
1) cloakroom 2) gallery
3) passage 4) hall

9

Animalier bronzes of Indians
and the 'Wild West' are
synonymous with the name of:
1) Stanley Orville
2) Rosa Bonheur
3) Frederic Remington
4) Antoine-Louis Barye

10

Three of these objects date from the C.17th, the fourth from the C.19th. Which is the odd man out:

1) *an iron rush light*
2) *a German grease lamp*
3) *a bronze pricket candlestick*
4) *a brass wall-sconce*

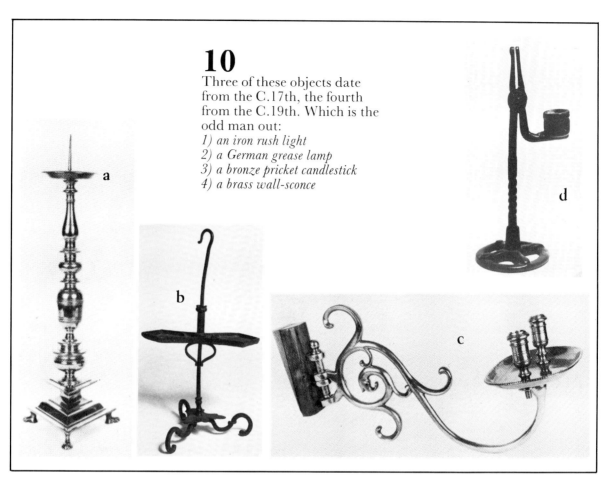

12

This allegorical bronze figure was made in:

1) France 2) Russia 3) Norway 4) Peru

11

This pair of Louis XV:

1) cassolettes 2) chenets
3) chiens de feu 4) girandoles

would have been placed on either side of:

a) an altar b) an alcove
c) a monument d) a fireplace

Tools

Whether it has been the growth of DIY or the increase of 'hi-tech' that has contributed to the growing interest in old tools it is impossible to say. The fact remains that antique tools of all kinds are attracting increasingly large numbers of collectors who are concerned as much with their decorative as their practical value.

In general, tools are, by their very nature, utilitarian; function dictating form in a manner that is very satisfying to the eye and to the touch. While even mass-produced tools of little age may display these qualities, it is undoubtedly the older tools which have the greatest appeal. These were often made by the craftsman for his own use – perhaps even while he was an apprentice – and, as such, no two are ever identical. Such tools will almost always have the owner's name punched or perhaps elaborately carved into them with, very often, a date as well. All of which adds hugely to their appeal – and probably their value as well.

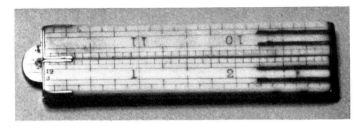

1

An ivory and nickel-plated brass foot rule such as this is worth:
*1) £5-10 2) £25-40 3) £80-120
4) £250-350*

2

These pre-1932 boxwood rules are by:
*1) Jack London 2) Samuel Paris
3) Edward Preston*

3

This is a bronze and steel:
*1) hatter's measure 2) T-square
3) try-square 4) depth gauge*

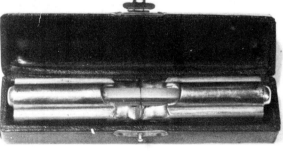

5

This spirit level would have been used by:
*1) a stonemason 2) a bricklayer
3) a paperhanger 4) an engineer*

4

This is a cast-iron:
*1) inlay cutter 2) veneer plane
3) spill plane 4) spoke shave*

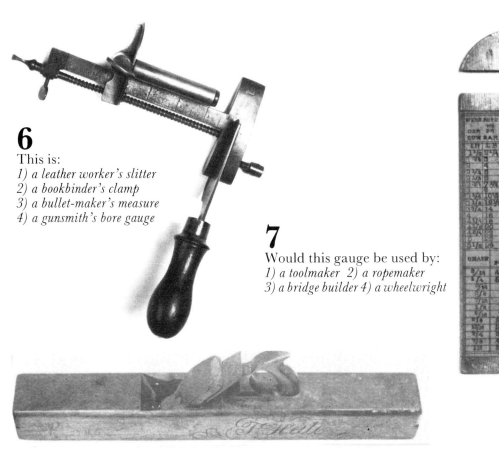

6

This is:
1) *a leather worker's slitter*
2) *a bookbinder's clamp*
3) *a bullet-maker's measure*
4) *a gunsmith's bore gauge*

7

Would this gauge be used by:
1) *a toolmaker* 2) *a ropemaker*
3) *a bridge builder* 4) *a wheelwright*

8

This is known as:
1) *a bench-plane* 2) *a jointing-plane*
3) *a trying-plane* 4) *a jack-plane*

9

This tool was used by an
C.18th:
1) *glazier* 2) *shipwright*
3) *cooper* 4) *cabinet-maker*

10

A hatter would have used this
for:
1) *pressing straw* 2) *curving wire*
3) *pressing ribbons* 4) *stretching
hats*

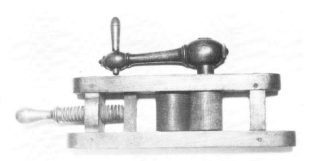

11

This is:
1) a hoe 2) a reaping-hook
3) an adze 4) a turf cutter

12

This side-axe was for use by:
1) a hurdle-maker 2) a coach-maker
3) a woodcutter 4) a shipwright

13

Hurdle-makers used this:
1) pickaxe 2) T-chopper
3) twybill 4) mattock

14

This is an Edwardian:
1) gardener's drill
2) stonemason's line
3) bricklayer's plumb
4) roofer's rafter gauge

15

Some tools have regional
variations. The pattern of this
hacksaw is from:
1) Kent 2) Midlothian 3) Dorset
4) Lancashire

16

This is:
1) a maul 2) a plumb bob
3) a tenon marker 4) a mortise gauge

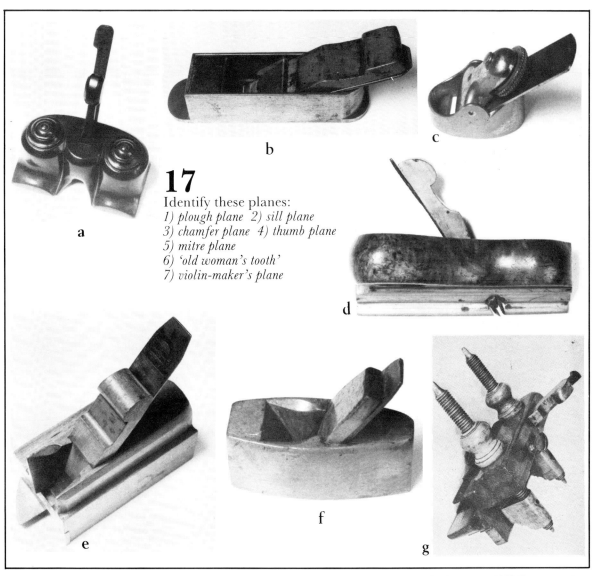

17

Identify these planes:
1) plough plane 2) sill plane
3) chamfer plane 4) thumb plane
5) mitre plane
6) 'old woman's tooth'
7) violin-maker's plane

a

b

c

d

e

f

g

18

This would have been used by
an C.18th:
1) gardener 2) plasterer
3) candle-maker 4) pastry-cook

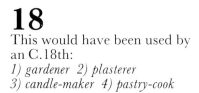

19

This would have been used by:
1) a glover 2) a saddler
3) a silversmith 4) a blacksmith

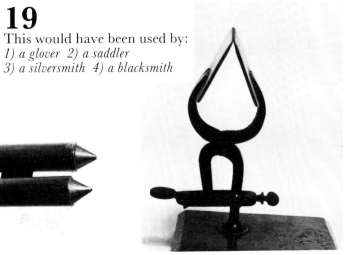

Guns

The history of firearms is a long one, with its roots in the Orient, and there is no question about the influence guns have had on the development of Western life.

Earlier examples, the works of individual craftsmen, tend to have wider appeal than the mass-produced relics of twentieth-century wars, but many modern sporting guns exhibit the same standards of individuality and excellence, often having been made to measure for wealthy and demanding customers.

Air guns, no less lethal under certain circumstances than firearms, also attract numbers of enthusiasts, and particular interest is shown in early examples but only if they are in working order.

The condition of any gun is an important factor in terms of value. Hard and durable as steel, its surface can be easily and permanently damaged by moisture and acid. To handle an unprotected gun barrel can subject it to both.

1

These are examples of guns with matchlock, wheel-lock and flintlock firing mechanisms. Which is which?

a   b   c

3

Would you call this:
1) a blunderbuss
2) an elephant gun
3) a repeater 4) a muzzle-loader

2

What date is this 16-bore percussion sporting gun:
1) c.1700 2) c.1840
d) c.1860 4) c.1910

4

What sort of gun is this:
1) a cap gun 2) an air gun
3) a shot gun 4) a water gun

5

How much would a pair of 8-bore wildfowling guns by Charles Lancaster be worth:
1) £800-1200 2) £1500-2000
3) £4000-6000 4) £8000-12000

Arms, Armour & Militaria

Although disproportionately large prices are sometimes paid by museums or international collectors for rare and important items, there is a healthy trade in the more everyday pieces. Specialist dealers and auctioneers are, perhaps, the best sources of information and advice for anyone wishing to buy and sell.

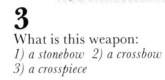

3
What is this weapon:
1) a stonebow 2) a crossbow
3) a crosspiece

1
What kind of cannon is this:
1) signal 2) siege
3) mortar 4) ship's

2
The part covering the hands on a suit of armour is called:
1) vambrace 2) greave
3) gauntlet 4) cuirass

4
What are these:
1) gunner's callipers
2) gunsmith's callipers
3) bore measures
4) bullet measures

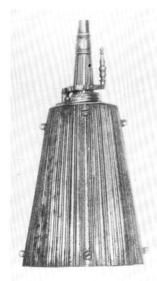

5
What is this:
1) a shot container
2) a flint holder 3) a powder flask
4) a powder horn

6
What date is this sword:
1) C.12th 2) C.13th
3) C.15th 4) C.18th

7

Was this sword made in:
1) Japan 2) China
3) Siam 4) Malaya

8

Is this a:
1) broadsword 2) rapier
3) sabre 4) dirk

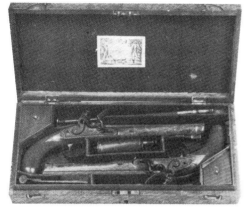

9

Would these pistols have been
used for:
1) hunting 2) signalling
3) target practice 4) duelling

11

This Italian C.16th helmet was
called a:
1) morion 2) firducce
3) stiletto 4) cowl

10

What is this officer's headgear
called:
1) a busby 2) a helmet
3) a parade cap 4) a bearskin

12

This suit of Japanese armour is
made chiefly of:
1) bamboo 2) iron 3) leather
4) papier mâché

13

What is this:
1) an axehead 2) a scimitar
3) a 'Ninja Star'
4) a piece of horse armour
What age is it:
a) c.1000 BC b) 10 BC
c) C.12th AD d) C.18th AD

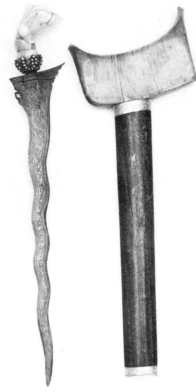

14

Is this:
1) a sceptre 2) a tipstaff 3) a mace
4) a bolus

15

What is this:
1) a poniard 2) a Sumatran kris
3) an assegai
4) a Samurai seppuku knife

16

This is 42 inches long. Is it:
1) a Chinese sword
2) a Japanese halberd
3) a machete 4) a cutlass

17

This Viking sword could be
described as:
1) showing its age 2) rusty
3) in excavated condition
4) distressed

18

Is this Bronze Age sword:
1) Spartan 2) Etruscan
3) Phoenician 4) Celtic

19

What is this:
1) a sword rest 2) a horsebit
3) a pair of shield ornaments
4) spurs

20

Is this:
1) halberd 2) sackbut 3) lance
4) axe
from the:
a) C.15th b) C.16th c) C.17th
d) C.18th

21

Are these medals for service in:
1) India 2) Africa
3) The Home Guard
4) The Fire Brigade

22

This early C.17th powder flask
is:
1) German 2) Indian 3) Bedouin
4) Italian

Toys

Once toys became desirable collectables after the Second World War, a great many people either remembered a particular childhood toy with affection and wanted another one or could now afford the toy that had eluded them.

One purchase led to another until, twenty years ago, collector interest was sufficiently established to warrant the London auction houses starting specialist sales. These sales in turn stimulated collector interest still further and prices started rising rapidly for toys which met the usual collecting criteria.

Interest in toys spilled over into other collecting areas, principally those which provided source material. A German wholesaler's catalogue, *c.*1877, depicting over 1000 lines and showing the transition from wooden to tinplate toys, was expected to realise £3000 but made over £18000.

If the toy collector was not spoiled in childhood, he certainly is now with swap-meets, collectors' clubs, specialist magazines, over fifty reference books to consult, half a dozen museums to visit and an original holiday destination in the Toy Soldier Museum in Tangier with its superb views of the Strait of Gibraltar.

1
What date is this doll's house:
*1) early C.17th 2) early C.19th
3) early C.20th*

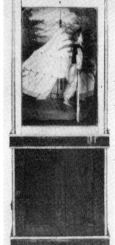

2
This clown gymnast is called:
*1) an automaton 2) a ganglion
3) a mechanical 'phizzer'*

3
What is the value of Mickey Mouse:
*1) £50-100 2) £200-250
3) £300-350 4) £400-500*

4

Where was this mechanical
money box made:
1) *Germany* 2) *USA*
3) *England* 4) *Ireland*

6

Was this tricyclist automaton
made in the:
1) *1870s* 2) *1880s* 3) *1890s*
4) *1900s*

5

Is this a:
1) *clockwork parachutist*
2) *construction doll*
3) *baby Houdini*

7

This 1930s' German model of
an R100 Zeppelin is worth
between:
1) *£50-100* 2) *£400-600*
3) *£600-800* 4) *£1500-2000*

8

Early C.20th teddy bears tend
to fetch very high prices. This
one sold in 1985 for:
1) *£50* 2) *£175* 3) *£300*
4) *£550*

Tinplate Toys

1
The earliest tinplate toys date from the:
1) 1820s 2) 1870s 3) 1900s

2
Where was this car made:
*1) Italy 2) France
3) Germany*
and when:
a) 1910 b) 1930s c) 1950s

3
This hand-painted car was made in 1910 by Carette. How much is it worth today:
*1) £100-200 2) £300-500
3) £2000-2500*

Models & Metal Toys

Hand finishing and attention to detail put ships and boats among the most expensive category of metal toys to produce and, because they were subject to sinking or straying, they are the most expensive now to buy.

In Nuremberg, Marklin, Bing and Carette all produced high-quality boats from the 1890s and an early twentieth-century Bing clockwork gunboat with original masts and rigging, 20 inches long, could sell for £750.

1
What was this used for:
*1) petrol 2) methylated spirits
3) lighter fuel*

2
These vans are early:
*1) Matchbox 2) Dinky
3) Dublo*
They are both worth around:
*a) £50-70 b) £100
c) £200-300 d) £400*

3

Which of these model trains is the most valuable:

a

b

c

4

This model car is desirable
because it is:
1) in good condition
2) the only one ever made
3) complete with box
4) 1 and 3

5

When would these soldiers
have been made:
1) 1850s 2) 1890s 3) 1920s

6

What is their value:
1) £50-100 2) £300-350
3) £1000-1500

7

These soldiers realised £660 at
auction. Was it because they
are:
1) South African 2) very rare
3) made of lead
4) 1 and 3 5) 1 and 2

8

When and where was this lorry
and trailer made:
1) c.1920   a) Italy
2) c.1945   b) France
3) c.1935   c) Germany

9

What is this machine:
1) an early vacuum cleaner
2) an hydraulic ram
3) a stationary steam engine
4) a dynamo

10

What is it:
1) a cylinder musical box
2) a phonograph
3) a gramophone
4) a crystal set

11

This bone model was made by:
1) prisoners of war
2) Chinese coolies
3) boy scouts 4) sailors
in the early:
a) C.18th b) C.19th c) C.20th

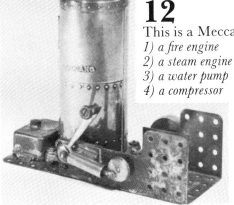

12

This is a Meccano model of:
1) a fire engine
2) a steam engine
3) a water pump
4) a compressor

13

Is this Noah's Ark:
1) German 2) French
3) South American

Dolls

Only when children were no longer considered as miniature adults did their need for playthings become generally accepted.

The earliest dolls were roughly carved from wooden pegs with crude attempts at articulation hidden beneath their clothing and until 1900 they always represented adult females, rarely baby girls or boys.

Few eighteenth-century dolls survive so that a peg-and-pivot joined doll with gesso-covered face and original clothes *c.*1735 has realised £18000 at auction.

1

A walking doll is sometimes called:
*1) an automaton 2) an auto-gear
3) an auto-peripatetikos*

2

How much is this C.18th doll worth:
*1) £10-20 2) £200-300
3) £1500-2000*

5

It is possible to date dolls according to the original clothes made for them – was this doll made in:
*1) 1810 2) 1850 3) 1890
4) 1910*

4

The most important part of the doll (besides the clothes) is the head. In the late C.19th it was most frequently made of:
*1) papier mâché 2) rubber
3) wax 4) bisque 5) 3 or 4*

3

The country which produced most dolls in the C.19th was:
*1) France 2) Italy
3) England 4) Russia*

Musical Instruments

The average price of a violin made by Antonio Stradivari of Cremona (1644-1737) is now £165,000 with exceptional examples selling to an amateur musician at £396,000 and to an American foundation for a professional musician to play at £286,000.

There is a growing field of thought among some musicians that Strads that have been in regular service are now past their best and no longer provide the desired edge. Hot favourite to succeed Stradivari is the nineteenth-century Italian violin-maker, Joseph Rocca of Turin, whose violins have increased in value from £15000 to £50000 since 1980.

1

Is this called a:
1) harpsichord 2) clavichord
3) spinet 4) short piano

2

This early C.19th fortepiano by John Broadwood is worth between:
1) £500-700 2) £1500-2500
3) £4000-5000 4) £10000-15000

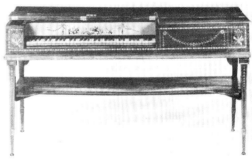

3

This type of piano is known as a:
1) table 2) cabinet
3) square 4) cottage
piano
When was it made:
a) c.1750 b) c.1790
c) c.1830 d) c.1900

4

This American:
1) Aeolian orchestrelle
2) pianola
3) Wurlitzer c. 1890
has rolls which are operated by:
a) electricity b) suction
c) pedals

5

Which of these gramophones is the earliest:

7

What sort of organ is this:
*1) chamber 2) miniature
3) cinema 4) barrel*

6

This whistle is used by a:
*1) scoutmaster 2) signaller
3) bosun 4) bosun's mate*

8

What is this:
*1) a black flute
2) a piccolo 3) pan pipes
4) a flute d'accord*

9

Is this:
1) *an English horn*
2) *a basset horn*
3) *a bent horn*
4) *a crumhorn*

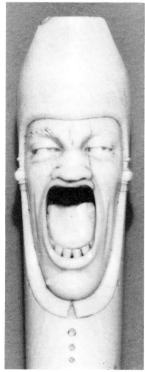

10

What is this:
1) *a flageolet*
2) *a recorder mouthpiece*
3) *a Swiss pipe*
4) *a stick flute*

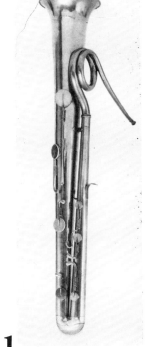

11

Is this an:
1) *ophicleide* 2) *orphicle*
3) *tremolo horn* 4) *saxophone*

12

What is this:
1) *a metronome* 2) *a violin bow*
3) *a spinet key*
4) *a drumstick*

13

What are these:
1) *Breton bagpipes*
2) *bladder pipes*
3) *Irish bagpipes*
4) *Northumbrian small pipes*

14
Is this:
1) a serpent 2) a bass horn
3) a bassoon 4) an alpenhorn

15
This upright piano is
sometimes called a:
1) harp piano 2) pianophone
3) giraffe 4) swan neck

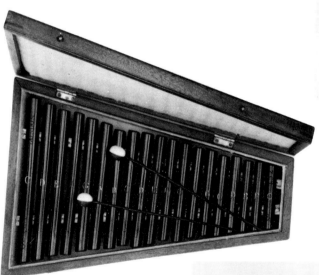

16
What is this:
1) a xylophone 2) a glockenspiel
3) a zither 4) tubular bells

17
What type of drums are these:
1) side 2) tenor
3) bass 4) kettle

Caddies & Boxes

Most boxes were originally made to fulfil a specific function and, of the best of these, perhaps the commonest are the writing slopes, vanity boxes and tea caddies. Of all the boxes, it is probably the latter which have shown the greatest changes with time.

The word 'caddy' is derived from the Malay 'kati', a unit of weight, equivalent to 1 1/5lb, by which tea used to be sold. The name was originally given to the porcelain jars in which tea was kept before the development of lockable wooden, ivory or tortoiseshell boxes known, in their early days, as tea chests.

Vanity boxes, like caddies, were originally supplied with interior fittings, and like caddies, are often found to have been plundered.

2

This 19-inch-wide box is dated *c*.1685. It is a:
1) bible box 2) candle box
3) jewel box 4) writing box

1

This 6-inch diameter box is known as a 'miser's':
1) groat box 2) purse 3) snuffbox
4) hump

4

Papier mâché objects were often inlaid with :
1) agate 2) brass 3) boxwood
4) mother-of-pearl

5

First to patent the papier mâché process in Britain was:
1) Henry Clay
2) Jennens and Bettridge
3) Charles Bielefeld
4) Thomas Chippendale
in:
a) 1652 b) 1772 c) 1786 d) 1830

3

This Reeves paint box dates from:
1) c.1880 2) c.1910 3) c.1925
4) c.1938

6

This box and contents were the property of:
*1) an alchemist 2) a conjurer
3) a witch 4) an explorer*

7

Behind the painted front of this 21-inch-high box are four drawers for:
*1) cigars 2) medals 3) socks
4) ammunition*

8

This gold and ivory box is for:
*1) jewellery 2) cutlery
3) writing materials 4) tea*

9

The decoration on this Austrian Art Nouveau jewel casket is typical of:
*1) Gustav Gurschner
2) Lucien Loetz
3) Siegfried Schmidt
4) Franz Hoosemans*

11

This box is 9½ inches long, decorated with mother-of-pearl; it is:
1) a collar box 2) a glove box
3) a pen box 4) a cigarette box

10

This is:
1) a medicine chest
2) a lepidopterist's cabinet
3) a barber's box
4) an apothecary's chest

12

This is a C.19th:
1) quill box 2) candle box
3) taper box 4) spill box

13

The original brasswork on this box suggests a date of:
1) c.1710 2) c.1790 3) 1810
4) 1890

15

A pyx is intended to contain:
1) holy relics 2) consecrated oil
3) communion wafers
4) a bishop's mitre

16

Of what material is this Regency tea caddy made:
1) glass 2) celluloid 3) agate
4) tortoiseshell

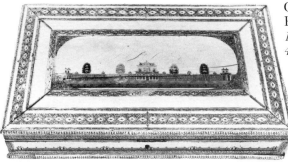

14

Ivory work-boxes with sandalwood linings are usually:
1) Anglo-Chinese 2) Anglo-Indian
3) Sino-Japanese

Ivory

Ivory, to a great many people these days, looks best where it belongs – jutting from the face of an elephant or walrus. The Victorians, however, thought otherwise and set off in vast numbers to prove their God-given superiority over the animal kingdom by slaughtering as many ivory/horn and fur bearing beasts as they could level a rifle at. Much of the resultant crop of ivory was converted into articles of jewellery, chess sets and figures of coquettish nymphs.

Following legislation reflecting increasing concern about wildlife conservancy, it is safe to say that there will be far less ivory coming on to the market in its raw state – and articles made of ivory will, in consequence, become increasingly rare. This should, in the normal way of things, cause the price of ivory to rise and multiply the number of fakes as more skilled workers in plastics discover new and profitable lines.

1

These are ivory:
*1) silk spools 2) patch boxes
3) travelling shaving brushes
4) salts*

2

What is the base of this candlestick called:
1) base 2) plinth 3) dais 4) socle

3

It is carved with:
*1) foliage 2) acanthus 3) lingzi
4) ferns*

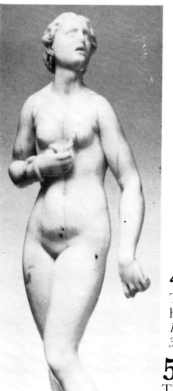

4

This ivory figure is carved holding a snake. She is:
*1) Eve 2) Lucrezia Borgia
3) Medusa 4) Cleopatra*

5

The small pinholes in her belly and thigh indicate:
*1) ivory worm 2) wilful damage
3) witchcraft 4) missing pieces*

6

This French ivory diptych leaf represents the Adoration of the Magi. It dates from which century:
1) 12th 2) 14th 3) 16th 4) 18th

7

It is carved in which style:
*1) Gothic 2) Renaissance
3) Pre-Raphaelite
4) Neo-Gothic*

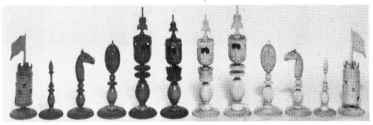

9

This Chinese figure was used:
1) as an ornament
2) as a paperweight
3) by a doctor
4) as an advertisement

8

This ivory tankard is probably:
1) Indian 2) Chinese 3) German
4) Japanese

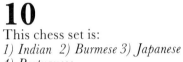

10

This chess set is:
1) Indian 2) Burmese 3) Japanese
4) Portuguese

11

These whale teeth are
decorated by a technique
known as:
1) acid etching 2) gravure
3) scrimshaw 4) tattooing

12

This is an Indian:
1) scent bottle 2) medicine bottle
3) powder flask 4) talisman

Enamel

The ancient process of decorating metalware with enamel was perfected in China and Japan in the seventeenth to nineteenth century, when designs would be inked on copper vases, overlaid with thin copper or silver wire to form partitions (cloisons), then filled with coloured enamels. The result, after firing, grinding and polishing, was a brilliantly coloured cloisonné vase, apparently made up of a mosaic of tiny enamel fragments.

Such pieces are extremely susceptible to damage, which dramatically reduces values of this and all enamel work.

2
This vessel is known as a :
*1) boat 2) kovzha 3) kovsh
4) tsarina*

3
It was made around the turn of the century in:
*1) Poland 2) Russia 3) Portugal
4) Sweden*

1
The coloured enamels on this vase are separated by means of copper wires. This technique is known as:
*1) cloisonné 2) champlevé
3) stringing 4) tôle peinte*

5
The enamels on this box are contained in indentations in the metal. This technique is known as:
*1) cloisonné 2) fielding
3) puddling
4) champlevé*

4
This enamel and gilt copper pyx was made in:
*1) Limoges 2) Dresden 3) York
4) Moscow*

6
It was made in the Jiayin year of Wanli of the Ming dynasty. In our calendar this corresponds to:
*1) 21 BC 2) AD 1349
3) AD 1614 4) AD 1872*

7

This is one of a pair of enamelled bronze objects 7½ inches in diameter. They are:
1) head bands 2) bell pulls
3) stirrups 4) napkin rings

8

This is:
1) a pipe
2) a carriage door handle
3) a bottle opener
4) a cane handle

12

This gold mounted enamel cigarette case was made in St Petersburg, 1896-1903, by:
1) Sazikov 2) Fabergé
3) Ovchinnikov 4) Khlebnikov

10

When was this candlestick made:
1) c.1725 2) c.1775 3) c.1850
4) c.1900

9

This silver gilt and enamel horn is:
1) Viennese 2) Parisian
3) Roman 4) Venetian

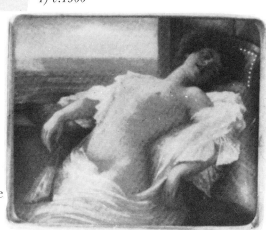

11

Where was this cigarette case made:
1) Germany 2) France
3) Italy 4) England

Treen

It is extraordinary how time can invest the humblest of objects with a value – and not only a financial value – far beyond anything its maker might ever have imagined.

Treen – the term used today to include any small, domestic wooden object (furniture generally excluded) – illustrates this point most clearly. In the main, treen, a word originally used to signify indigenous wood, was used to make simple, cheap and durable utensils such as bowls, spoons, drinking or measuring vessels as – and often by whom – they were needed. Accordingly, quality of craftsmanship varies considerably, but even the most simply made item has an appeal scarcely to be matched by a modern equivalent.

Besides the rustic pieces, we now include many quite finely turned items of exotic timbers and even mass-produced souvenirs such as Mauchline ware and small decorative items of Tunbridge ware.

1
This is a Tunbridge ware:
1) music stand 2) book rest
3) display stand

2
Tunbridge ware was made:
1) in Tunbridge Wells
2) in Tonbridge
3) by Richard Tunbridge
4) in Tonbridge Road, Birmingham

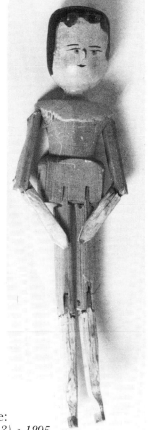

3
This doll was made:
1) c.1750 2) c.1810 3) c.1895
4) c.1925

4
This is a treen:
1) honeypot cover 2) beehive
3) money box 4) string box

5
This is:
1) a handkerchief dryer
2) an adjustable wig stand
3) a wool winder
4) a stocking stretcher

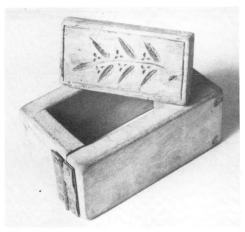

6

This is a beech:
1) brick mould 2) butter mould
3) printing block

7

These are:
1) a condiment set 2) desk sanders
3) cosmetic pots 4) string holders

8

This is a wooden:
1) water bottle 2) pendulum weight
3) powder flask 4) shot flask

9

The pierced decoration on this
candle box is known as a:
1) club 2) cloverleaf 3) trinity
4) trefoil

10

This silver-mounted pot is
made of:
1) ebony 2) lignum vitae
3) coconut shell 4) gourd

11

This is a boxwood:
1) *dice shaker* 2) *toddy cup*
3) *measure* 4) *eggcup*

12

This candlestick dates from:
1) *c.1750* 2) *c.1800*
3) *c.1850* 4) *c.1900*

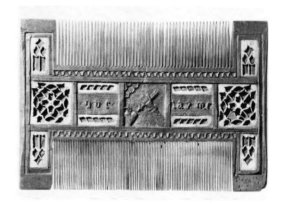

13

This bread board would be
worth:
1) *£1-5* 2) *£10-15* 3) *£20-30*
4) *£35-50*

14

This wood and bone comb is
French. It was made:
1) *c.1480* 2) *c.1620* 3) *c.1790*
4) *c.1830*

15

In perfect condition it would
be worth:
1) *£10-15* 2) *£30-50*
3) *£1000-1500* 4) *over £2500*

16

This snuffbox is carved from:
1) *walnut* 2) *coquilla nut*
3) *boxwood* 4) *maple*

17

This string and wood 'ruler' is:
1) *Indian* 2) *African*
3) *Japanese* 4) *Russian*

Kitchenalia

1

Match the caption to the illustration:

1) chocolate moulds
2) pastry jiggers
3) scarifier
4) trug
5) nutmeg grater
6) carcass stretcher
7) eel trap
8) oyster opener
9) butter worker
10) knife cleaner
11) slicer
12) larkspit
13) coffee grinder
14) feeder
15) potato masher
16) cutlery tray

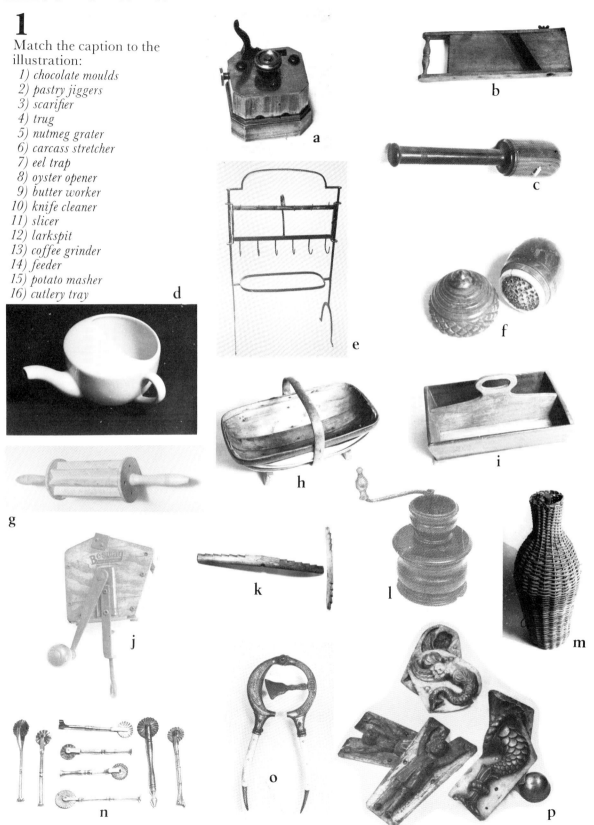

2

What sort of iron is this:
1) flat 2) smoothing
3) box 4) goffering

3

This iron was heated:
1) on the stove 2) with charcoal
3) with a hot iron slug
4) with boiling water

4

This is a Chinese:
1) saucepan 2) water ladle 3) iron
4) tea measure

5

What were these used for:
1) cutting sugar 2) boning meat
3) removing horseshoes
4) trimming shoe leather

6

Is this:
1) a bottle-jack 2) a garlic press
3) an angelica press 4) a nutcracker

7

What is this:
1) a cocoa tin 2) a block chocolate
grater
3) a chocolate dispenser
4) a hot drink machine
What date:
a) 1900s b) 1920s c) 1930s
d) 1940s

8
What decorative influence is here:
*1) Modernist 2) Art Nouveau
3) Art Deco 4) Functionalist*

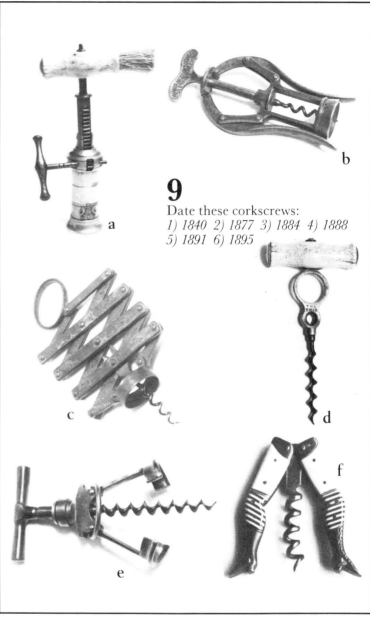

9
Date these corkscrews:
*1) 1840 2) 1877 3) 1884 4) 1888
5) 1891 6) 1895*

a

b

c

d

e

f

10
Wicker was often used for small baskets in conjunction with which other wood:
*1) oak 2) beech 3) willow
4) alder*

11
What is this:
*1) a potato masher
2) an isinglass mixer
3) a batter whisk
4) a cream whisk*

Transport

The years between 1890 and 1896 saw a bicycling boom, possibly encouraged to some extent by the introduction of the first ever HP scheme by the Raleigh Company of Nottingham. Soon thereafter, as cars went into mass production, cycling lost its appeal.

The interest in collectable cars is these days divided roughly into two camps: the car as a piece of engineering history, and the car as a one-time possession of a famous person, particularly if that person was one of the stars of the entertainment world.

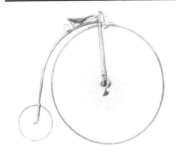

1

This:
1) velocipede 2) dandyhorse
3) penny farthing 4) bone-shaker
is worth:
a) £100-150 b) £300-500
c) £600-800 d) £1300-1600

2

What sort of carriage is this:
1) hackney cab 2) landau
3) barouche 4) omnibus

3

Is this:
1) a 1931 Austin Seven saloon
2) a 1926 Morris Ten saloon
3) a 1934 Panhard Tourer
4) a 1933 Austin Ten drophead
   saloon

4

What did this:
1) Aston Martin 2) Ferrari
3) Bentley 4) Porsche

cost new in England in 1965:
a) £1500 b) £2630
c) £4412 d) £6725

5

What is this:
1) a motorbike 2) an autocycle
3) an autoped 4) a moped

6

What is this:
1) a landaulette
2) a victoria
3) an invalid carriage
4) a governess cart

Textiles/Costume

Seeking refuge for his troubled soul some 1500 years ago, St Mungo entered a cave in the bank of a burn where he saw a dazzling light illuminating the face of a little child 'clothed in a soft fair robe of exceeding fineness like unto white-spun gossamer'.

In years to come, the cave was to become Glasgow Cathedral and the soft white robe the model for the Ayrshire whitework christening robes made in Scotland between 1815-70.

Ayrshire whitework consists of embroidering in white thread on white muslin graceful sprays of flowers into which small areas of needlepoint are incorporated. In 1837, some 20,000 pieceworkers were employed at 'flowering' by the Glasgow manufacturers.

Ayrshire whitework was neglected by collectors for many years as being neither embroidery nor lace, but in common with other articles of costume the handwork was exquisite and practically impossible to duplicate nowadays.

1

This type of C.17th raised needlework is called:
1) crewelwork 2) petit point
3) gros point 4) stumpwork

2

This panel is composed of:
1) needlework 2) glass beads
3) barbola 4) jet beads

3

This is an Italian:
1) bedspread 2) altar frontal
3) portière 4) valence

4

What is this needlework panel called:
1) an 'ABC' 2) a needlewoman
3) a sampler 4) a template

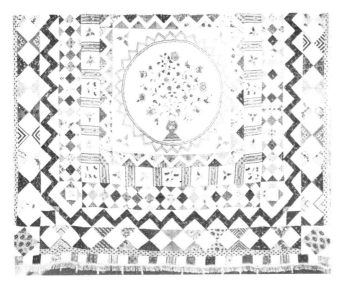

6
This tapestry is:
1) Dutch 2) Flemish
3) German 4) French

5
This coverlet is made in:
1) brocade 2) appliqué
3) patchwork 4) crewelwork

8
What is this·
1) a lady's nightcap
2) a tea cosy
3) a glove cover
4) a gentleman's nightcap

7
What date are these gloves:
1) c.1500 2) c.1620 3) c.1750

9
What period is this bonnet:
1) 1720s 2) 1800s
3) 1840s 4) 1880s

Is it made of:
a) straw b) leather
c) cotton d) lace

10
What date is this 'open robe':
1) c.1650 2) c.1700
3) c.1760 4) c.1820
How much is it worth:
a) £500-800 b) £1000-1200
c) £5000-6000 d) £10000-14000

11

This type of shawl was very popular in the 1860s. It was made in which part of India:
1) Kashmir 2) Punjab
3) Seringapatam 4) Bombay
This pattern was also made in which Scottish town:
a) Dunbar b) Glasgow
c) Paisley d) Aberdeen

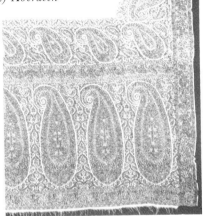

12

Is this robe:
1) Japanese 2) Chinese
3) Indian
4) North American Indian

13

What do these four rugs have in common:
1) they are all runners
2) they have geometric patterns
3) they are prayer rugs
4) they have diaper patterns

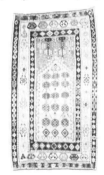

14

This carpet comes from which famous French manufactory:
1) Lyons 2) Savonnerie
3) Aubusson 4) Sèvres

15

What is the popular name for
this shape of rug:
1) runner 2) passage
3) alley 4) hall

16

This panel was made in:
1) Turkestan 2) Afghanistan
3) Bokhara 4) Samarkand

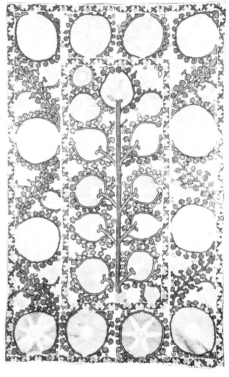

17

This type of rug is called a:
1) prayer 2) tent
3) floor 4) dhurrie

18

This rug was made in:
1) Kurdistan 2) Persia
3) Arabia 4) Bessarabia
and is worth between:
a) £500-800 b) £1000-1500
c) £3500-4500 d) £6000-9000

Miscellany

Small miscellaneous items have a nasty habit of getting lost, which is distressing for the owners at the time, but can sometimes be most rewarding for the finders centuries later. Take for example the latest safety device fitted to all AD 50 model chariots – a bronze horn cap. If a charioteer racing along at speed fell out, he would need one to haul himself back in again.

Inconvenient for the charioteer who lost his near present-day Cromer, but rewarding for the farmworker who found it. It made £12960 at auction.

Lost in the River Nene, an 11-inch diameter bronze dish used for ritual washing before confession was identified as a rare Romanesque 'Hansa' dish. It may well have been used for 400 years until the Reformation and then dumped as too incriminating. In any event, it netted the finder £11000.

1

What sort of spoon is this:
1) jam 2) mincemeat 3) caddy
4) pickle

2

This pair of pots was made in the reign of which king:
1) George I 2) George II
3) George III 4) George IV

3

These boxes decorated with a mosaic of tiny pieces of wood are called:
1) Bathware 2) Tunbridge ware
3) Pembroke ware 4) Pontypool

4

What is it:
1) a flare holder 2) a rattle
3) a plumber's probe
4) a glove stretcher

5

This type of elaborate ivory carving is associated with which French town:
1) Toulon 2) Lille
3) Reims 4) Dieppe

6

Fit the caption to the
illustration:
*1) vinaigrette 2) wine label
3) letter scales 4) pipe tamper
5) tinder pistol 6) plaster mould
7) butter pats 8) stay busk
9) coat hooks 10) head measurer
11) cat*

a

b

c

d

e

f

g

h

i

j

k

7

Is this perambulator:
1) late Georgian 2) Regency
3) mid-Victorian 4) late Victorian

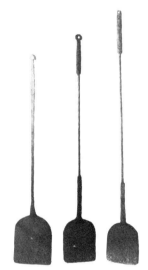

8

When was this tricycle built:
1) c.1790 2) c.1830 3) c.1885
4) c.1904

9

Is this a:
1) generator 2) knife-grinder
3) nail sharpener 4) lathe

10

Where would you find these
tools, in a:
1) grocers 2) bakers
3) chandlers 4) chemist

11

These C.17th Flemish carvings
are of:
1) city fathers 2) Apostles
3) prophets 4) fruit-growers

12

Worn Sheffield plate reveals
which metal underneath:
1) copper 2) pewter 3) cadmium
4) brass

13
These candlesticks are by Kayserzinn, notable Art Nouveau producers of:
1) lustreware 2) wood 3) brass
4) pewter

14
Who would have used this brass basin:
1) a barber 2) a gynaecologist
3) a surgeon 4) a dentist
5) 1 and 3

Is it:
a) a shaving basin
b) an instrument tray
c) a bleeding bowl d) a leech dish
e) a and c

15
This is a lacemaker's:
1) cushion 2) chest 3) pillow
4) creel

16
What is this silver-plated object:
1) an ear trumpet
2) an opium pipe
3) a baby feeder
4) a drinking fountain spigot

17
What is this mid C.19th object:
1) a veterinary douche
2) a stethoscope
3) a balloonist's oxygen tube
4) a conversation tube

18

This is a mechanical:
1) warning siren 2) fire bellows
3) water pump 4) sausage-maker

19

This small hand vice would
have been used by:
1) a silversmith 2) an angler
3) a surgeon 4) a cabinet-maker

20

What is this iron object:
1) a Christmas tree stand
2) a flagpole stand
3) a doorstop
4) a rifle rest

22

John Lennon's handwritten
lyrics for 'Imagine' sold at
Sotheby's in 1983 for:
1) £75 2) £1250 3) £6600
4) £10800

21

Made of brass, this has
connections with:
1) the orchestra 2) the sea
3) waste disposal 4) firefighting

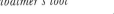

23

In ancient Egypt this wooden
handled bronze object was:
1) a mirror 2) a winnowing fan
3) a cooking utensil
4) an embalmer's tool

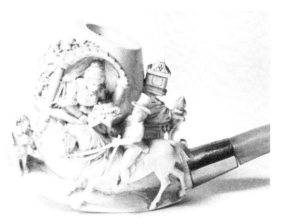

24
This pipe is carved out of a soft stone called:
1) *soapstone* 2) *meerschaum*
3) *mollstein* 4) *doucette*

25
This is a Gecophone. What was it for:
1) *seismic measurement*
2) *radio reception* 3) *electrolysis*
4) *electrical generation*

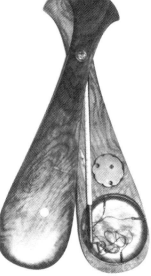

27
For what were these Chinese scales used:
1) *tea* 2) *gold* 3) *opium* 4) *spices*

26
This C.19th ewer is made of:
1) *boxwood* 2) *ebony* 3) *porcelain*
4) *ivory*

28
This small round object is:
1) *an early tennis ball*
2) *a model of Mars*
3) *an early golf ball* 4) *a pomander*

29

What substance is this mould
used for:
1) chocolate 2) glass
3) gutta-percha 4) lead

30

This light fitting is in which
style:
1) Art Nouveau
2) Functionalist 3) Modernist
4) Art Deco

32

Is this globe:
1) celestial 2) terrestrial
3) astrological 4) navigational

31

Is this:
1) a chastity belt
2) an orthopaedic corset
3) an instrument of torture
4) a falconer's hat

33

What principle does this
machine demonstrate:
1) electrolysis 2) electric capacitance
3) sound reproduction 4) gyroscopics

Competition

WIN AN ANTIQUE

£5000 worth of antiques to be won

First prize – an antique or antiques worth £2500
Second prize – an antique or antiques worth £1500
Third prize – an antique or antiques worth £1000

What you have to do

Answer the ten questions on pages 147 and 148. Write your answers clearly on the entry form in the space provided. Then complete the sentence on the reverse of the entry form, beginning *'I always watch The Antiques Roadshow because . . .'* in not more than twenty-five words. Add your name, address and post code and send your entry to The Antiques Roadshow Quiz Book Competition, Sissinghurst Court, Sissinghurst, Cranbrook, Kent TN17 2JA, to arrive not later than 1 November 1986.

How to get your prize

Prizewinners may choose their antiques from a dealer, shop or auction house of their choice anywhere in the United Kingdom, Northern Ireland or the Republic of Ireland. Winners will be accompanied by a member of the BBC who will make the purchases for them.

Rules of Entry

Entries must be on a proper entry coupon cut from the Antiques Roadshow Quiz Book and must bear the entrant's own name and address. All accepted entries will be examined, and the judges will award the first prize to the entrant who has correctly answered the ten questions and who, in the event of a tie, is judged to have submitted the most compelling, original and best expressed reason for watching The Antiques Roadshow. Remaining prizes will be awarded for next best attempts in order of merit, and no entrant may win more than one award. Prizes must be accepted as offered – there can be no alternative awards, cash or otherwise.

Entries arriving after the closing date will not be examined and no responsibility can be accepted for entries lost or delayed in the post or elsewhere. Any entries received incomplete, illegible, mutilated, altered or not complying with the instructions and rules will be disqualified.

Decisions of the judges will be final. No correspondence will be entered into. Entry implies acceptance of the rules as being final and legally binding.

The competition is open to all readers aged 18 and over in Great Britain, Northern Ireland and the Republic of Ireland except employees and their families of the BBC, Chilston Publications, associated companies of either of them, or anyone else directly involved with the competition.

Winners will be notified and the results will be announced during the course of the 1987 series of The Antiques Roadshow. A list of prizewinners can be obtained by sending a stamped, addressed envelope to The Antiques Roadshow Quiz Book Competition Results, BBC Publications, 35 Marylebone High Street, London W1M 4AA.

1

This tiny oriental carving of a flautist (3.6 cm high) was made early C.19th and probably used as a button. What is this type of carving known as?

2

This German silver gilt snuffbox is apparently unmarked (except for a C.19th control mark). What price did it fetch at a New York sale in 1984? (Give price to nearest $100.)

3

Which famous C.20th architect designed this chair and stool?
What is the name of the design?

4

What is this 6½-inch-high pear-shaped beech object?

5

What is this?

6

These high-heeled shoes of ivory silk embroidered in silver thread and lined with kid were made in which part of C.18th:
1) early 2) mid 3) late

7

What type of carriage is it?

9

The back of this chair is characteristic of which C.18th furniture designer?

8

This walnut mantel clock has a French movement with an outside count wheel striking on a bell. The clock is 25 inches high and was made towards the end of the C.19th. Where was it made?

10

This percussion truncheon/pistol is made from brass and has a cast eagle-head pommel. It was made in London. Circa when? (To the nearest 5 years.)

Answers

Beds (pages 18-19)
1) **3**
2) **3**
3) **1**
4)   *The bed on the left is a C.19th tester bed, the other a C.17th example.*
5) **2&a**
6) **3**
7) **1**   *A half tester, so called because the roof does not extend to the full length of the bed.*
8) **2**   *A Regency ormolu lit en bateau. Much furniture of the period shows Empire influence.*
9) **4**   *A cupboard bed. It folds away behind its own cupboard doors.*

Bookcases (pages 20-21)
1) **3**
2) **1**
3) **2**   *'Breakfront' simply means that the line of the front of the piece is broken by a projecting centre section.*
4) **3**   *A George III mahogany breakfront secretaire bookcase.*
5) **4**   *Either term is acceptable.*
6) **2**
7) **3**
8) **2**
9) **3**
10) **2**   *A style adapted from classical buildings.*
11) **3**

Bureaux (pages 22-24)
1) **2**   *A mid C.18th mahogany bureau.*
2) **1**   *A mid C.18th mahogany kneehole desk.*
3) **3**   *A mahogany partners' desk c.1790.*
4) **3**

5) **1**   *So called after André Charles Boulle, 1642-1732.*
6) **4**   *A Carlton House writing table c.1810. Said to derive its name from a pattern supplied to Carlton House, residence of the then Prince of Wales.*
7) **2**   *So called after a Captain Davenport, said to have placed the original order with Gillows of Lancaster.*
8) **1**   *A late C.18th satinwood bonheur du jour of English manufacture.*
9) **1**
10) **2**
11) **3**   *An early C.20th oak roll-top desk.*
12) **1c**   *A Queen Anne walnut bureau.*
    2d   *An Edwardian mahogany veneered bureau.*
    3b   *A Queen Anne walnut bureau-on-stand.*
    4a   *A George I walnut bureau.*

Cabinets (pages 25-28)
1) **1b**   *A Queen Anne lacquer cabinet-on-chest.*
    2d   *A George I walnut secretaire cabinet.*
    3c   *A Sheraton satinwood dressing cabinet c.1795.*
    4a   *An Art Nouveau mahogany display cabinet c.1900.*
2) **4**
3) **4**   *A Victorian mulberry veneered folio cabinet c.1855.*
4) **1**   *An Art Nouveau mahogany cabinet in the manner of Charles Rennie Mackintosh c.1890.*
5) **5**   *Late C.18th, satinwood.*
6) **3&d**   *A Chippendale-style piece c.1800.*
7) **4**   *A satinwood and inlaid piece c.1800.*
8) **2**   *An elaborate inlaid cabinet in the manner of Robert Adam c.1770.*

9) **2&a**   *A Regency cabinet c.1820.*
10) **3**   *A George III mahogany corner cabinet c.1760.*
11) **2**   *A 'Chinese Chippendale' lacquered cabinet c.1760.*
12) **1**   *A mid-Victorian marble-topped walnut credenza.*
13) **2&a**   *These cabinets are still being reproduced by robbing earlier pieces.*
14) **3**   *A C.19th Chinese cabinet of carved padouk wood.*

Chests (page 29)
1) **2**   *Camphorwood has a distinctive figure. Sometimes found to have been painted.*
2) **2**   *An English oak chest c.1500.*
3) **1**
4) **3**
5) **2**   *From its appearance, which resembles folds of linen.*
6) **4**   *The most durable of English woods.*

Chairs (pages 30-35)
1) **1e**   *Claw and ball foot.*
    2d   *Scroll foot.*
    3c   *Lion's paw foot.*
    4f   *Cabriole leg.*
    5g   *Pad foot.*
    6b   *Spade foot.*
    7h   *Blind fret.*
    8a   *Sabre leg.*
2) **3**   *A George III water-gilded side chair.*
3) **a**   *Cresting.*
   b   *Splat.*
   c   *Arm.*
   d   *Seat.*
   e   *Seat-rail.*
   f   *Knee.*
   g   *Scroll foot.*
   h   *Stretcher.*

i		Upright.
j		Finial.
4)	**4**	
5)	**3**	
6)	**1c**	Tub.
	2b	Fiddle-back.
	3a	Ladder-back.
	4e	Chinese fretwork.
	5i	Winged.
	6h	Thrown.
	7j	Cane.
	8d	Shell.
	9f	Interlaced.
	10g	Rococo.
7)	**3**	
8)	**4&c**	A Regency metamorphic library chair c.1800.
9)	**1**	A Louis XV chaise longue.
10)	**2**	A late C.18th painted beechwood armchair.
11)	**2**	A Kohn 'Fledermaus' armchair designed by Josef Hoffmann c.1907.
12)	**4**	
13)	**1**	
14)	**2**	A C.19th Welsh pine lambing chair.
15)	**4**	A Dutch marquetry cockfighting chair c.1730-40.
16)	**1**	An English parcel gilt mahogany master's chair c.1730.
17)	**1**	
18)	**2**	
19)	**3**	
20)	**1**	
21)	**1**	

Settees, Sofas & Couches
(pages 36-37)

1)	**3**	
2)	**1c**	A Louis XV walnut sofa.
	2d	A Louis XVI giltwood sofa.
	3a	A Regency rosewood sofa.
	4b	An American mahogany sofa c.1850.

3)	**1**	
4)	**3**	
5)	**3**	A Louis XV duchesse en bateau.
6)	**4**	An Edwardian wicker settee.
7)	**4**	

Chests of Drawers & Commodes
(pages 38-40)

1)	**1d**	Mid C.17th.
	2b	George I.
	3a	Early George III.
	4c	Early C.19th.
2)	**a**	Demi-lune.
	b	Bombé.
	c	Serpentine.
	d	Bow-front.
3)	**2**	
4)	**1**	
5)	**3**	
6)		English c.1760.
7)	**1a**	A Louis XV marquetry bow-fronted commode.
	2c	An early Louis XV kingwood bombé commode.
	3b	A Louis XV transitional commode.
	4d	A Louis XVI mahogany commode.
8)	**1**	
9)	**2**	
10)	**4**	English c.1760.
11)	**2**	A George I walnut bachelor chest.
12)	**3**	
13)	**2**	A Louis XV semainier, with seven drawers, one for each day of the week.

Cupboards & Wardrobes
(pages 41-43)

1)	**4**	
2)	**2**	
3)	**1**	

4)	**4**	A mid C.17th oak hanging cupboard.
5)	**1a**	A Welsh oak hanging cupboard c.1670.
	2e	A Louis XVI provincial oak armoire.
	3b	A Dutch C.18th floral marquetry press.
	4c	A George III mahogany gentleman's wardrobe.
	5d	An C.18th/19th Welsh pine linen press.
	6f	A 'Mouseman' oak wardrobe by Robert Thompson, 1930s.
6)	**2**	
7)	**3**	A George III mahogany bedside cupboard.
8)	**4**	
9)	**3**	
10)	**2**	Note the elaborate brass escutcheons and 'H' hinges.
11)	**4&c**	Carved and inlaid. Value £1500-2500.

Tables (pages 44-47)

1)	**2**	A Henry VII oak trestle table.
2)	**1c**	A marquetry Pembroke table.
	2e	A late George II mahogany silver table c.1760.
	3a	A Regency rosewood and parcel gilt console table.
	4b	A giltwood side table.
	5d	A sewing table.
	6f	A George III mahogany card table with blind fret decoration.
3)	**1**	
4)	**4**	
5)	**4**	
6)	**2**	English, mahogany, c.1740.
7)	**3**	A Regency mahogany table.
8)	**1**	
9)	**3**	
10)	**3**	A late C.18th giltwood and scagliola table of neo-classical design.
11)	**4**	A Victorian papier mâché work table with mother-of-pearl decoration.

12) **2&a**   *English, late C.18th.*
13) **a**   *A Regency mahogany whatnot.*
    b   *A George II mahogany dumb-
waiter.*
14) **3&b**
15) **1f**   *A pedestal dining table.*
    2d   *A penwork games table.*
    3c   *A Victorian walnut centre
table.*
    4e   *A draughtsman's kneehole
table.*
    5b   *A Sheraton tricoteuse.*
    6a   *A library table.*
    7g   *A kettle stand.*
16) **3**   *An early C.19th envelope table.*
17) **3&a**

Dressers & Sideboards (page 48)
1) **3**
2) **1**
3) **1c**   *A Lancashire pine dresser.*
    2a   *An Irish pine dresser.*
    3b   *A Cornish pine dresser.*
4) **2**   *This is a reproduction, as are
virtually all in this style. No
genuine example will ever be
found in such good condition,
since these were actually used
to keep chickens in.*
5) **3**

Miscellaneous Furniture
(pages 49-51)
1) **2&b**
2) **3**   *A C.17th beech bread trough of
pegged construction.*
3) **1b**   *A mahogany coalbox c.1900.*
    2e   *A mid-Georgian mahogany
bottle stand.*
    3c   *A plate rack.*
    4a   *A wine cooler.*
    5d   *A George III mahogany
cellaret.*
    6f   *A canterbury.*

4) **3&a**
5) **4**
6) **3**   *English, C.17th/18th.*
7) **1**   *A George I walnut linen press.*
8) **3&d**   *A George III Irish mahogany
peat bucket.*
9) **4**   *A Regency rosewood fire-screen
with hinged reading flap and
sliding panel.*
10) **2**   *An Indian footstool (chowkie)
inlaid with ivory, early C.19th.*
11) **3**   *A George III black and gold
japanned torchère c.1765.*
12) **2**   *A George II mahogany stand
with later marble top.*
13) **1**
14) **2**   *A Victorian pine washstand
with cutout for basin.*
15) **2**   *A Bagshaw and Sons fitted
dressing table with
silver-topped cut-glass bottles
and ivory-backed brushes.
Value around £1500.*

Mirrors (page 52)
1) **1**
2) **3&b**
3) **4**
4) **4**
5) **3**
6) **3**   *A Queen Anne burr walnut
toilet mirror c.1710.*

Ceramics (pages 53-65)
1) **3**
2) **2&a**
3) **3**
4) **1**
5) **3&b**
6) **3**   *A delftware salt c.1730.*
7) **2**
8) **2&a**
9) **3&c**   *Liverpool flower bricks c.1760.*
10) **2**

11) **3**
12) **1**   *A Worcester blue and white
egg-cup.*
13) **3&a**
14) **1**
15) **3**
16) **1g**   *A Derby ice pail c.1794.*
    2e   *A pastille burner c.1835.*
    3c   *A Longton Hall sauceboat.*
    4h   *A Worcester cress dish and
stand.*
    5a   *A Chamberlain's Worcester
honey pot.*
    6d   *A spill-vase.*
    7b   *A Worcester sifter spoon.*
    8f   *A Derby tureen.*
17) **2**
18) **4**
19) **1&c**
20) **3**
21) **3**
22) **2**   *Transfer printing resembles
an etching, the picture being
made up of fine lines with no
areas of solid colour.*
23) **1**
24) **3**
25) **2**
26) **3**
27) **3**
28) **3**
29) **2**
30) **3**
31) **4**
32) **4**
33) **3**
34) **4&a**
35) **4**
36) **3**
37) **4**
38) **1**
39) **3**
40) **2**
41) **1c**   *A nécessaire.*
    2h   *A bodkin case.*
    3g   *A chestnut basket.*
    4b   *A cane handle.*
    5d   *A thimble.*
    6a   *A scent bottle and stopper.*
    7i   *A pipe bowl.*

8f   *A cheese dish.*
9e   *A foot bath.*
42) **4**
43) **1**
44) **3**
45) **3**
46) **2**
47) **1**
48) **3**
49) **2**
50) **1**
51) **2**
52) **1**
53) **4**
54) **3**
55) **4**   *Specially made for the BBC TV programme* Jim'll Fix It. *European c.1880. It is a Meissen pagoda figure after a model by J. J. Kaendler.*
56)
57) **1**
58) **3**
59) **2**
60) **4**
61) **1**
62) **4**
63) **4**
64) **1**
65) **1&b**
66) **3**   *Zsolnay was famed for stylised figures and lustre finishes.*

Clocks & Watches (pages 66-71)
1) **3**
2) **1**   *A late Queen Anne walnut longcase clock by Daniel Quare.*
3) **4**
4) **4**   *An ebonised, double-basket top bracket clock by Brouncker Watts.*
5) **3**   *An eight-day longcase clock by John Knibb. Longcase is the correct name for the grandfather or grandmother clock.*
6) **4**

7) **1**   *A late Georgian mahogany balloon bracket clock.*
8) **2**
9) **3**
10) **1d**   *A late Stuart marquetry bracket clock.*
   2g   *An ebony bracket clock c.1725-50.*
   3e   *A Louis XV gilt bronze mantel clock c.1760.*
   4f   *A Haley and Milner ebonised bracket clock c.1795.*
   5a   *An Empire ormolu mounted mantel clock.*
   6c   *An ormolu bracket clock of Louis XV style, made c.1825-50.*
   7b   *A late Victorian oak and ormolu bracket clock.*
11) **1a**   *Garniture.*
   2d   *Lighthouse clock.*
   3b   *Lyre clock.*
   4c   *Mantel chronometer.*
12) **3**
13) **2**
14) **4**
15) **3**
16) **1d**   *Cuckoo clock.*
   2b   *Sedan clock.*
   3e   *Lantern clock.*
   4c   *Act of Parliament clock.*
   5a   *Stopwatch.*
17) **1**   *A mystery because the hands turn by no immediately discernable means.*
18) **4**
19) **3**
20) **1**   *A variety of clocks were made with 'spires' resembling those of notable cathedrals.*
21) **2&d**
22) **1c**   *A German early C.17th verge watch.*
   2a   *A silver pair-cased verge watch early C.18th.*
   3e   *A pair-cased verge watch with nautical dial 1779.*
   4d   *A mid C.19th open-faced pocket watch.*

   5b   *A hunting cased stopwatch.*
23) **4**   *A silver, triple-cased watch by Edward Prior, London.*
24) **3**
25) **2**
26) **2**
27) **3**
28) **2**

Scientific Instruments
(pages 72-75)
1) **3**
2) **1**   *The compass engraved with twelve signs of the zodiac.*
3) **2**
4) **3**   *A W.&S. James opaque solar microscope late C.18th.*
5) **3&b**   *By Troughton and Sims mid C.19th.*
6) **1**
7) **2**   *A brass miner's dial signed 'Walter, Dublin' 1792.*
8) **3**
9) **2**   *A Place & Co. amputation set, English mid C.19th.*
10) **1**   *A set of six dental hygiene instruments with bone toothbrush.*
11) **3**   *C.19th iron delivery forceps.*
12) **3**
13) **3**   *A C.19th walnut cased stick barometer by L. Casella.*
14) **1**   *A Georgian clock/barometer by John Bond.*
15) **2&a**   *A Thomas Harris mahogany way-wiser early C.19th.*
16) **4**
17) **3**
18) **3**   *A Jesse Ramsden double frame sextant c.1798.*
19) **1**   *An English silver perpetual calendar.*
20) **2**   *A late C.18th brass telescope by Troughton.*
21) **2**

Photographic (page 76)
1) **3**
2) **1**
3) **4**
4) **2**
5) **5**

Silver (pages 77-83)
1) **1a**   *Cake basket.*
  2d   *Tea caddy.*
  3e   *Epergne.*
  4c   *Castor.*
  5i   *Invalid feeder.*
  6h   *Chalice.*
  7g   *Argyle.*
  8k   *Centrepiece.*
  9f   *Soap box.*
  10b   *Wine coaster.*
  11j   *Soup tureen.*
2) **3**
3) **3&b**
4) **1d**   *Marked 1705.*
  2c   *Marked 1719.*
  3b   *Marked 1736.*
  4a   *Marked 1763.*
  5e   *Marked 1931.*
5) **1**
6) **3**
7) **4**
8) **1**
9) **1**
10) **4**
11) **4**
12) **3**
13) **1a**   *1839.*
  2c   *1911/12.*
  3d   *1938.*
  4b   *1956.*
14) **2**
15) **3&b**
16) **4**
17) **2&c**
18) **2&b**
19) **1d**   *York.*
  2b   *Birmingham.*
  3a   *Sheffield.*
  4c   *Edinburgh.*

  5e   *Dublin.*
20) **1d**   *King's.*
  2e   *Queen's.*
  3a   *Fiddle Thread.*
  4c   *Hourglass.*
  5b   *Fiddle Thread and Shell.*
21) **2**
22) **4**
23) **a**   *The other three are Georgian.*
24) **1**   *By Jan Diederik Pont, Amsterdam 1757.*
25) **2**   *An Elizabeth I silver gilt seal-top spoon by William Cawdell, London 1598.*
26) **2**

Glass & Paperweights (pages 84-88)
1) **3&c**
2) **2**
3) **1&d**
4) **3**
5) **3**
6) **2**
7) **1**
8) **2**
9) **3**
10) **4**
11) **1**
12) **2**
13) **3**
14) **1**
15) **4**
16) **2**
17) **2**
18) **4**
19) **2**
20) **3&c**
21) **1&c**
22) **3**
23) **2**
24) **3**
25) **4**
26) **4**
27) **1**
28) **4**
29) **3**
30) **2**

Art Nouveau/Arts & Crafts (pages 89-93)
1) **4**   *Designed by George Jack for Morris & Co.*
2) **2**   *A mahogany buffet.*
3) **3**
4) **1**   *An Art Nouveau mahogany display cabinet c.1910.*
5) **3&a**
6) **3**
7) **3**
8) **4**
9) **1&c & iv**
10) **3&c**
11) **3&b**
12) **3**   *A Tiffany Favrile vase, engraved and moulded.*
13) **4**   *After Auguste Caïn.*
14) **4**
15) **3**
16) **2**   *Painted by Frederick Passenger in ruby lustres on white.*
17) **1**   *A Doulton, Lambeth vase incised by Hannah Barlow and Frank Butler 1878.*
18) **3**
19) **2**   *A silver cased mantel clock marked for Birmingham 1910.*
20) **2**   *By George Tinworth.*
21) **4**   *'Spring' – one of a set of the four seasons.*
22) **2**
23) **1**   *Made in Birmingham 1905.*
24) **4**
25) **1**
26) **3**   *A Foley 'intarsio' vase c.1900.*
27) **2**

Art Deco (pages 94-98)
1) **3**   *A silver tea set by Emile Viner, Sheffield 1938.*
2) **1**
3) **3**
4) **2**
5) **2**   *A Fritz Hansen laminated wood armchair, Danish.*
6) **4**
7) **2&c**
8) **2**   *A Cartier cigarette case, 1954.*

9) **3**

10) **4&c**   *A Preiss figure 'The Archer' 1930s.*

11) **2**   *'Girl on Wall' early to mid-1930s.*

12) **3**

13) **2&c**

14) **4**   *Naiades, by Lalique.*

15) **1&b**

16) **3**

17) **3**

18) **4**   *A Lalique glass knife rest 1920s.*

19) **4**   *'Source de la Fontaine'.*

20) **4**   *Of pale amethyst glass with chromed light mount.*

21) **1**   *Valued in America, in 1984, at around $2000.*

22) **3**

23) **2**   *By Bruno Brevette, France.*

24) **3**   *Designed by Oscar Gundlach-Pedersen, 1930s.*

25) **3**

Metalware (pages 99-101)

1) **3**   *By Johann Heinrich Giese, mid C.18th.*

2) **1**   *A spiked cast-iron mantrap c.1880.*

3) **4**   *A Nuremberg brass alms dish.*

4) **3**

5) **1**

6) **2**   *A bronze skillet of 7 inches diameter.*

7) **3**

8) **4**   *A George III gilt bronze hall lantern c.1760.*

9) **3**

10) **1d**

11) **2&d**   *A pair of late Louis XV bronze and gilt chenets c.1770.*

12) **1**

Tools (pages 102-105)

1) **2**   *Made by Edward Preston.*

2) **3**

3) **2**   *By Holtzapffel, 12 inches long.*

4) **3**   *7 inches long, Edward Preston.*

5) **4**   *In velvet-lined box, worth £15-25.*

6) **1**   *Made of brass and steel, by James Dixon, Sheffield.*

7) **2**

8) **3**   *28 inches long, worth £80-100.*

9) **4**   *A large French rebate-plane dated 1752, 45 inches long and worth £200-300.*

10) **1**   *C.19th, worth £30-40.*

11) **3**   *A wood shaping tool, 31 inches long.*

12) **2**

13) **3**   *Made by a C.19th Kentish blacksmith.*

14) **1**

15) **4**

16) **4**   *Of ebony and brass.*

17) **1g**   *Of beech and boxwood, brass mounted.*

    2d   *Of walnut and boxwood.*

    3e   *Chamfer plane.*

    4f   *Boxwood, 3 inches long.*

    5b   *A steel mitre plane by Moon, 145 St Martins Lane, c.1800, worth £200-300.*

    6a   *'Old woman's tooth'.*

    7c   *Brass, late C.19th, worth £50-60.*

18) **3**

19) **1**

Guns (page 106)

1) **a**   *A German wheel-lock gun early C.17th.*

   b   *An Italian flintlock sporting gun late C.18th.*

   c   *A Dutch matchlock target gun late C.17th.*

2) **2**

3) **1**   *An Italian flintlock blunderbuss c.1740.*

4) **2**   *A pump-up air gun late C.18th.*

5) **4**

Arms, Armour & Militaria (pages 107-110)

1) **1**   *A Victorian cannon with bronze barrel.*

2) **3**   *A duelling gauntlet c.1630.*

3) **2**   *A sporting crossbow C.17th.*

4) **1**   *C.19th by Elliot Bros, London.*

5) **3**   *An Italian, all-steel powder flask early C.17th.*

6) **3**   *A medieval sword found in the Thames C.15th.*

7) **1**   *A Shinto tachi.*

8) **3**   *A Georgian sabre c.1800.*

9) **4**

10) **1**

11) **1**   *A Brescian morion late C.16th.*

12) **2**   *Early C.18th armour with earlier (1584) helmet.*

13) **1&a**   *A Luristan bronze axehead.*

14) **3**   *A German seven-flanged mace mid C.16th*

15) **2**   *A gold-mounted kris with a hippopotamus ivory handle.*

16) **1**   *Inscribed with emperor's name and dated 1840.*

17) **3**   *A Viking-type sword of the C.9th.*

18) **4**   *Late 2nd millennium BC.*

19) **2**   *A Luristan bronze horsebit c.1000 BC.*

20) **1&b**

21) **4**

22) **1**

Toys (pages 111-112)

1) **2**

2) **1**   *An electrically operated automaton, English c.1925.*

3) **4**   *Plush covered, 20 inches high.*

4) **2**   *A cast-iron money box, the head hinged to deposit a coin placed in its mouth into the food trough. Late C.19th.*

5) **1**   *German, c.1938.*

6) **2**   *A French bisque-headed automaton.*

7) **3**
8) **4**

Tinplate Toys (page 113)
1) **2**
2) **2&b**   *A C.I. J., tinplate and clockwork Alfa Romeo racing car.*
3) **3**

Models & Metal Toys
(pages 113-115)
1) **3**   *A British 'Fillalita', penny-operated fuel dispenser.*
2) **2&d**
3) **c**   *Worth £1000-1200.*
4) **4**   *A near mint condition car c.1935, worth £450-550.*
5) **2**
6) **2**
7) **5**
8) **3&c**
9) **3**   *A single-cylinder steam engine.*
10) **1**   *Swiss c.1840.*
11) **1&b**
12) **2**
13) **1**   *c.1920.*

Dolls (page 116)
1) **3**
2) **3**   *A George III wooden doll, late C.18th, repainted early C.19th.*
3) **1**   *A Henri Lioret phonograph Jumeau doll, French c.1893.*
4) **5**   *A bisque doll, French c.1880.*
5) **2**   *A swivel-head bisque doll, French c.1850.*

Musical Instruments
(pages 117-120)
1) **3**   *An English 'bent side' spinet inscribed Gulielmus Rock, C.18th on later stand.*
2) **3**
3) **3&b**
4) **1&c**

5) **e**   *A Gramophone Company horn gramophone c.1908.*
6) **4**
7) **4**   *A late C.19th Continental barrel organ playing ten airs on three locks.*
8) **4**
9) **2**
10) **2**
11) **1**
12) **3**
13) **4**
14) **1**
15) **3**
16) **2**
17) **4**

Caddies & Boxes (pages 121-123)
1) **3**   *An C.18th 'miser's' table snuffbox in burr yew.*
2) **1**   *A mahogany bible box.*
3) **2**
4) **4**   *A papier mâché writing box with fitted interior, c.1850.*
5) **1&b**
6) **3**
7) **1**   *An oak 'sentry box' cigar cabinet of four drawers, English, c.1910.*
8) **4**
9) **1**   *Gurschner is best known for domestic decorative bronze objects.*
10) **4**   *Complete with bottles and glass mortar. English mid C.19th.*
11) **3**   *Fitted with pen-tray and glass inkwell c.1904.*
12) **2**
13) **1**
14) **2**   *Typical C.19th work.*
15) **3**
16) **4**

Ivory (pages 124-125)
1) **1**   *Dating from c.1820.*
2) **4**   *The term 'socle' is applied to any turned base made as a separate piece.*

3) **2**   *A popular decorative motif in the C.18th.*
4) **4**   *South German early C.17th.*
5) **4**   *There would originally have been some drapery across her loins. Ivory is frequently pegged and glued together.*
6) **2**
7) **1**
8) **3**   *Typical German work, second half C.19th.*
9) **3**   *Chinese doctors would not examine female patients, but would ask them to indicate centres of discomfort on such figures as this, c.1900.*
10) **1**   *A red and natural ivory Delhi chess set early C.19th.*
11) **3**   *Beware of resin fakes and replicas!*
12) **3**   *Made of ivory plaques pinned onto a wooden liner late C.18th.*

Enamel (pages 126-127)
1) **1**   *A Chinese vase, Qianlong.*
2) **3**
3) **2**
4) **1**   *C.13th.*
5) **4**
6) **3**   *A rare, dated champlevé box and cover.*
7) **3**   *Reputedly worn by the Duke of Schomberg at the Battle of the Boyne in 1690, where he fell in action. Made at Esher, Surrey, between 1649 and 1684.*
8) **4**   *A silver gilt and enamel cane handle by Rudolf Linke. Late C.19th.*
9) **1**   *By Rudolf Linke.*
10) **2**   *One of a pair of Bilston enamel candlesticks and trays c.1775.*
11) **1**   *A typical piece of German erotica from the 'naughty nineties'.*
12) **2**   *Owned by Prince Juan Faleo di Savoia, Ambassador of Spain to Russia 1887-91.*

Treen (pages 128-130)
1) **2**   *A rosewood book rest c.1860.*
2) **1**   *The museum at Tunbridge Wells, Kent, contains a fine display of this C.19th decorative work.*
3) **3**
4) **4**   *Boxwood c.1840.*
5) **3**   *A late Victorian wool-winder.*
6) **2**
7) **2**
8) **1**
9) **4**   *A C.19th wall-hanging candle box.*
10) **3**
11) **1**   *Boxwood C.18th.*
12) **2**
13) **2**   *Value varies according to quality and condition of carving.*
14) **1**
15) **4**   *An extremely rare item.*
16) **2**   *An early C.19th coquilla nut snuffbox. Coquilla nut is sometimes called 'vegetable ivory'.*
17) **3**   *A C.19th lumi tsubos.*

Kitchenalia (pages 131-133)
1)   **1p**   *Chocolate moulds.*
     2n   *Pastry jiggers.*
     3a   *Scarifier.*
     4h   *Trug.*
     5f   *Nutmeg grater.*
     6k   *Carcass stretcher.*
     7m   *Eel trap.*
     8o   *Oyster opener.*
     9g   *Butter worker.*
     10j   *Knife cleaner.*
     11b   *Slicer.*
     12e   *Larkspit.*
     13l   *Coffee grinder.*
     14d   *Feeder.*
     15c   *Potato masher.*
     16i   *Cutlery tray.*
2) **3**
3) **2**
4) **3**   *A late C.19th brass pan iron with ivory handle.*

5) **1**   *Georgian wrought steel sugar nips.*
6) **4**
7) **3&c**   *A Menier chocolate dispenser, French.*
8) **3**
9) **1a**   *1840.*
     2d   *1877.*
     3c   *1884.*
     4b   *1888.*
     5e   *1891.*
     6f   *1895.*
10) **3**
11) **4**

Transport (page 134)
1) **3&c**
2) **2**
3) **1**   *In near-original condition.*
4) **1&c**   *Sold in 1983 for £5000.*
5) **3**   *A motorised scooter c.1916.*
6) **3**

Textiles & Costume (pages 135-138)
1) **4**   *A C.17th stumpwork panel.*
2) **2**   *A fine beadwork panel, English mid C.17th.*
3) **2**   *Dated 1620. Florentine.*
4) **3**
5) **3**
6) **2**
7) **2**   *Made of beige kid.*
8) **4**   *Dated c.1600.*
9) **3&a**
10) **3&c**
11) **1&c**
12) **1**
13) **3**
14) **3**
15) **1**
16) **3**
17) **4**
18) **4&c**

Miscellany (pages 139-145)
1) **3**

2) **3**

3) **2**
4) **2**
5) **4**
6)   **1a**   *Vinaigrette.*
     2b   *Wine label.*
     3e   *Letter scales.*
     4g   *Pipe tamper.*
     5h   *Tinder pistol.*
     6f   *Plaster mould.*
     7i   *Butter pats.*
     8d   *Stay busk.*
     9j   *Coat hooks.*
     10k   *Head measurer.*
     11c   *Cat.*
7) **2**
8) **2**
9) **4**
10) **2**
11) **2**
12) **1**   *A Sheffield plate candlestick c.1790.*
13) **4**
14) **5&e**
15) **3**   *Continental.*
16) **1**
17) **4**   *The tube 84 inches long, with silver-plated trumpet and ivory ear tube. English mid C.19th.*
18) **2**   *Cast-iron and brass bellows. English late C.19th.*
19) **2**   *A C.19th fly-tying vice.*
20) **1**
21) **2**   *A late C.19th brass manually operated foghorn.*
22) **3**   *c.1971. Material of this kind is attractive to the faker.*
23) **1**   *Of the 18th dynasty.*
24) **2**   *c.1870.*
25) **2**   *A crystal set of the early 1920s.*
26) **4**
27) **3**
28) **3**   *A white-painted, feather-filled golf ball. Sold in 1984 for £750.*
29) **3**   *It is a golf ball mould.*
30) **3**   *A Perzel chromium-plated lamp c.1930-5.*
31) **2**   *Late C.18th, steel, and most uncomfortable.*
32) **1**
33) **3**

157

36